Origins

of Modern

Sculpture

W. R. Valentiner

Wittenborn and Company,
New York, 1946

The publishers and author acknowledge
their indebtedness to all persons and institutions
mentioned in the list of illustrations.

Manufactured in the United States of America
by E. L. Hildreth and Company, Brattleboro, Vermont.

First edition

Jacket, binding and typographical format by Paul Rand

Preface:

In preparing the following notes, I tried first to find help in books on the history of sculpture and on aesthetics, but I soon discovered that very rarely even an attempt has been made by historians to explain what, in their opinion, constitutes a good piece of sculpture. The philosophers have treated the subject very casually, and often in a manner befitting the time of Lessing's *Laocoön* rather than our own.

After searching in vain through the literature on the subject, I decided to note down, in a rather haphazard way, observations I had made during my study of old and modern sculpture — without trying to make out of this an aesthetic system, for which I am not qualified.

That interest in the problems of sculpture is great at the present time is proved by the fact that several books on the subject have been published while I worked on mine. When I read these books after I had finished my manuscript, I was astonished to discover in how many different ways a problem can be treated.

Generally these books deal either with modern or with old sculptures — or with modern sculpture and such works of an earlier period as are related to modern art. No attempt has been made, I believe, to find a common formula for old and modern sculpture, a formula that must exist. By old art, I mean in this instance the art of the so-called realistic epochs, like that of Greece and Rome, and Western art from the fifteenth to the nineteenth century. It is, of course, comparatively easy to find similar formulas for modern art and for certain phases of mediaeval, early Oriental and prehistoric art. But it seems to me unfair to throw overboard the art of the epochs in between. In these periods, undoubtedly, great sculptors lived, although they may be of less interest to our time, sculptors like the Hellenistic masters, those of the High Renaissance and the Baroque from Michelangelo to Bernini and Rodin. To leave out these epochs would mean also to dispose of nineteenth-century American sculpture, which, although of no great importance in general history, must be studied if we want to understand the trend of modern sculpture in this country.

I should mention, however, two publications which seem to me of fundamental importance for the understanding of modern sculpture: Moholy-Nagy's *The New Vision* (1937)[1] and C. Giedion-Welcker's *Modern Plastic Art* (1937). Both authors go further in developing modern ideas than I have tried to do in the present book, which leads only to the doorsteps of abstract art. Those who want to enter what is still to many a temple of mystery should not fail to study these two small volumes.

What position abstract art holds in the complete aspect of our time no one can as yet tell. Some, with good reason, believe it to be the art of the future. This would mean that sculpture which deals mainly with the human figure in a realistic manner, and sculpture which expresses *actual* instead of *virtual* volume, is an art of the past, never to return. The conclusion is tempting, because it seems to result logically from the development of sculpture during the last decades. Once before in history, sculpture (the term is here used in the traditional sense) came to an end, after the decline of the ancient world, an epoch which has often been compared to ours. From about the fourth to the tenth century A.D. there existed hardly any sculpture of the human figure, either in Europe or in the Near East. It was replaced by an abstract plastic art of rare refinement — we may take as examples the façade of Mschatta in Syria, the transennas in early Christian churches at Rome and Ravenna, the stone monuments and metal objects in Ireland.

Yet it is dangerous to derive analogies from so short an experience as the history of mankind affords. We have witnessed, thus far, only two complete developments in the field of sculpture: the first, from archaic

1. Third revised edition, 1946.

art (about the seventh century B.C.) to late Roman art (about the fourth century A.D.); the second, from the Middle Ages to our time (c. 1000–1900). In both instances the development proceeds along similar lines. It starts with the closed form bound to architecture in primitive art and advances to the open form in late pictorial sculpture. This is comparable to the flower which is first closed as a bud, then opens slowly until the petals are spread out in all directions; when the petals have fallen, a long period of rest ensues, before the cycle begins again. This happened at the end of the first historical phase of sculpture, at the end of Roman art.

The second phase starts around the year 1000, with the closed forms of early mediaeval sculpture and develops towards the open forms of late Gothic and Baroque art which lead finally to Rodin and from there — if we believe in the victory of abstract art — to Calder. The counter-movements expressed in the sculpture of Maillol and his contemporaries of the last generation, who again stressed the closed form, would then represent a recurrent wave of short duration, which frequently appears in the final stages of a development, as for instance at the time of Constantine, when sculpture unexpectedly followed a trend towards the compact style of the pre-classical period.

Although we may not feel certain about a dominant position for abstract art at the present time, we may go so far as to say that it assumes a definite place in the decorative arts of today. Every period of originality has had its particular forms of decoration. The Middle Ages had stained glass windows, mosaics, enamels, tapestries, all of which it was impossible to imitate at any later time. The fact that mobiles, wire sculptures, transparent constructions of plastics and other kinds of modern technics are used increasingly for decorative purposes in modern homes shows that we have at last found fields of decorative art that are characteristic of our time. In saying this, we do not intend to depreciate their artistic value. It was not until the nineteenth century that theoretically inclined art historians differentiated between major and minor arts, while in the Middle Ages those who provided objects of decorative art were considered as great as painters and sculptors.

If a reactionary future, however, should prove that abstract art in its new form will have lasted but a comparatively short period, those who have been accustomed to deride it should not conclude that its ephemeral value will thus have been confirmed. Such a development would mean merely that the intensity of emotions brought about by the incredible experiences of the two wars, and in consequence producing an art of great visionary conceptions, has lessened. Great art, like steel, will be formed only under pressure of intense heat. Only an epoch in which mankind has suffered to a degree unparalleled in history could stimulate an art which turns the eyes away from battlefields towards spheres where stars alone hold sway. And only those who have never been carried away by the beauty of pure cosmic elements may doubt that abstract art can become the highest spiritual expression, as it has in our time — an expression that will elevate man as long as the experience of great art exists.

There is only one excuse for writing a book like the present one, which deals with problems of which very few have been settled by common opinion — that the author feels deeply about the subject and for this reason believes it worth while attempting to communicate to others the happiness he has received from it. There are still too many sceptics among us who see nothing but confusion in the efforts of present-day artists and who do not think it necessary to bother to disentangle the confusion. We are fully aware that nothing is more dangerous for the younger generation than scepticism, a return to unbelief and an adherence to the fallen gods of the past, because it was precisely this attitude that created the atmosphere most favorable to war. We must look forward, and we ought to feel proud of what has been achieved within a short time in building up a new pattern of life after the old idols have been smashed. In what messages should we believe if not in those of the artist, who stands above the world, devoting his life to the study of the eternal laws of nature and who sees the future with the intuition of the prophet?

Table of Contents

List of Illustrations

Chapter I

Painter and Sculptor

Part I

Leonardo the painter; Michelangelo the sculptor

In an age of over-refined culture, Leonardo da Vinci discussed the comparative value of the arts of painting and of sculpture and came to the conclusion that painting was the greater of the two. Michelangelo, in answering him, came to the opposite result, comparing the art of sculpture to the sun, the art of painting to the moon.

Such a dispute seems foreign to us nowadays, because we feel the incongruity of a comparison between two completely different fields of artistic expression, which are of equal importance in the history of mankind. But it is worth while to listen to the strange discussion of the two greatest masters of the High Renaissance, as it not only throws light upon their personalities, but also reveals some of the typical characteristics of the sculptor and the painter. We expect both Leonardo and Michelangelo to be excellent judges of the art of painting as well as of the art of sculpture, since they worked in both mediums, even though the first was preeminently a painter, the second preeminently a sculptor.

Leaving aside for the moment the particular argument, which in the end did not prove much one way or the other, we find the manner in which it was presented characteristic of the two types of artists. The discussion was rather one-sided, as Michelangelo was too temperamental to discuss anything seriously. While Leonardo loved to elaborate his points and repeated them in different form over and over again, Michelangelo, who had not the other's philosophical mind, answered only because he felt that he was being attacked.

"In discussing such matters," he said, "one loses one's time. I could finish a piece of sculpture in the meantime." With this he probably alluded to Leonardo, whom he once — without being asked — reproached to his face for not being able to finish his equestrian statue — very unjustly, for Michelangelo himself suffered from leaving most of his commissions unfinished. He showed his worst side when it came to disputes between equals. He became annoyed and insulting, for his nature was all emotion. "He who said that painting is higher than sculpture is as ignorant as my maidservant," he wrote to a friend, again alluding to Leonardo.

Their different temperaments

Leonardo was too well balanced to express himself so rudely to an adversary. He was all intellect, lacking the passionate temper which constantly caused Michelangelo trouble. Their manner of working revealed the same difference.

1

One of Leonardo's arguments in favor of the superiority of painting was that the painter can do his work in orderly clothes, in clean surroundings, noiselessly, even listening to music, while the sculptor becomes dusty and dirty and pursues his laborious work in the midst of terrific noise (Figs. 1, 2).

It is true that Michelangelo lived in a very disorderly fashion in filthy living quarters, as we are told by Paolo Giovio. He was extremely unsocial, for he did not care to have anyone near while he worked, and he worked all the time. Leonardo, on the other hand, was almost too orderly, too well dressed for an artist and too much inclined to communicate his ideas to others or to formulate them for his diary.

Orderliness is a sign of a composed style of life. It means constant self-control, an attitude ruled more by intellect than by emotion. Michelangelo had none of these qualities. His works were produced out of a volcano of wild emotions and fits of flaming scorn and despair. The result is that they touch us more directly than do those of Leonardo, whose very dreams were logical and intellectual and whose fundamental aim was an all-embracing knowledge of the universe.

Intellectual qualities of the painter, emotional ones of the sculptor

If we compare, in the Louvre, the *Mona Lisa* of Leonardo (Fig. 3) with the two *Slaves* of Michelangelo (Fig. 4), we find that the first affects us more intellectually, the second more emotionally. The bodies of the sculptures are so vibrating with life, so directed to our sense of touch, that we feel almost physically the pain they are suffering. There is nothing of this sensuous nearness to life in Leonardo's portrait. The *Mona Lisa* impresses us with her intellectual superiority, shown in her face with the high forehead, the wise eyes, the indefinable smile, in the poise and dignity of her attitude, and the grandness of nature surrounding her. She is very distant from us, her body is veiled, not alone by garments, but more by an impenetrable mystic atmosphere. The longer we look at her, the more she seems to move away from us into the vast space of the cosmos. The longer we look at Michelangelo's figures, the nearer they come to us, until in sympathy we identify ourselves with them.

If we compare other works by these masters, even those which are least appealing, for instance, the *Leda* of Leonardo (Fig. 5) and the *Resurrected Christ,* in the Minerva, by Michelangelo (Fig. 6), the fundamental difference of temperament becomes still more apparent. Leonardo's *Leda,* marvelously as the composition is calculated, leaves us cold; we expect a greater nearness to life from so sensuous a subject, although not necessarily the exaggerated sensuality of Michelangelo's treatment in his late cartoon (Fig. 7). The conception of Michelangelo's statue of Christ

2

does not fit the subject any better. This voluptuous body, presented to us in a most skilfully twisted pose, is disturbing to many people. We turn to the face, expecting a compensation, but Michelangelo's heads are subordinated to their bodies, their subconscious, half-drowsy expression corresponds to the heavy limbs they crown. In an effort to give vividness and spirituality to the head of Christ, the artist succeeded only in expressing an empty sweetness, which is in keeping with the thick-necked, athletic type of the figure.

It is logical that Leonardo's Christ from the *Last Supper* became the prototype of Christ for many thinking Christians, while Michelangelo's Virgin of the *Pietà,* in St. Peter's, became that of the consoling Madonna for the unhappy masses. The head of Leonardo's Christ, of which the body can only be guessed, is transparent and serene; it has the far-away spiritual look which we expect in him in his departing hours. But Michelangelo's Madonna, less spiritual with her enormous body grounded in the earth, appears to us in her vast garments like a protecting mother who draws us to her by the pitiful gesture of her outstretched hand.

If we are right in supposing that the works of two outstanding masters of the High Renaissance, Leonardo and Michelangelo, are good examples of what a painter and what a sculptor can express with his means during an age of realistic art, it seems that those of the sculptor have a greater nearness to life, affect us more emotionally and sensuously, while those of the painter have a more distant, dreamlike quality, of greater intellectual import. By this we do not mean to say that the sculptor will always be sensuous, the painter always intellectual. There are many sensuous painters, and there are, also, intellectual sculptors, although probably not as many in proportion, for reasons we shall explain.

As a rule, those painters by nature strongly sensuous or strongly emotional are more inclined than intellectual painters to produce exaggerated sculptured forms, expressed either in the design or in the material used. For instance, Rubens' sensuality expresses itself in a very plastic style, especially in his earlier work; Rembrandt and van Gogh — both painters whose emotional intensity increases towards the end of their lives — develop in later years a pasty, plastic technique, moulding the forms as it were with their hands, so that they appear to have a substantial, earthy quality. On the other hand, painters of cool temperament and intellectual character like Leonardo, Vermeer and Whistler prefer a smooth, almost invisible technique. Leonardo's technique is so invisible that it is impossible to see in his paintings that he was left-handed, a fact that is very conspicuous in his drawings. And the perfect evenness of Vermeer's technique has been a riddle to many observers who have tried to penetrate the subtlety of his procedure.

If our observation in regard to intellectual painters is correct, we should find that intellectual sculptors would come nearer to painting in their conception than emotional ones do. We must remember, however, that this kind of sculptor is very rare, because, on account of the physical exertion required by the execution of plastic works, the sculptor will generally be by nature a robust, even an athletic person — and it is usually conceded that a highly developed intellect and physical strength are seldom found together. The notion of a physically weak sculptor is almost a contradiction in itself, while there have been many great painters who were of delicate constitution. It is hardly accidental that many well-known sculptors throughout history reached a very old age; for instance, Claus Sluter, Ghiberti, Luca della Robbia, Donatello, Michelangelo, Houdon and, in our time, Rodin, Maillol, Kolbe, Barlach — most of them worked into their eighties. The two best American sculptors of the nineteenth century, Thomas Ball and John Quincy Adams Ward, both reached the age of eighty. This is not because sculpturing is a very healthy activity, although it is probably more so than painting, but because these artists would not have turned to sculpture if they had not been physically fit for the strenuous labor required.

In spite of this, we may perhaps say that those early sculptors who, by the fact that they were able writers, proved to be of intellectual nature, like Ghiberti, Leonardo, Cellini, practised a manner of sculpture more closely related to painting than the sculptors of more emotional nature, like Donatello or Michelangelo. The same can be said of modern sculptors: Rodin, who in spite of his deep emotions was obviously of an intellectual nature compared with Maillol, is much more pictorial in his style than Maillol. His intellectuality spoiled many of his later works, in which he tried to express ideas possible of expression only in painting, while Maillol, a much narrower mind, never overstepped the limits of sculpture.

Part 2

Actual form in sculpture, abstractions of form in painting

If nature had provided us with only one eye, as the Cyclops, we should see everything in the flat, and in walking we should have difficulty in measuring distance. In this case, painting, instead of sculpture, would probably have been the first of all arts, as it deals with reproducing an external world upon a flat surface. Since we have two eyes, we see the world around us as the plastic form of which it consists. Whatever we see has

4

volume: the table at which we sit, the room that surrounds us, the earth, the stars. Sculpture is a translation of the plastic forms around us into one concentrated form, a minute representation of the form of the earth itself, or at least of the forms which the earth has produced. To create a piece of sculpture is thus a much more direct and fundamental process than to create a painting, which means to translate a vision we have seen in the resemblance of volume and of space upon a flat surface. Sculpture translates one form into another, painting translates real forms into the abstractions of forms.

Different processes in creating sculpture and painting

The different materials employed by sculptor and painter show that painting as it is practised nowadays is the product of a highly civilized state of man, while sculpture is still produced with comparatively primitive means. Sculptures are formed with the hands out of clay, are cut with knife or with chisel out of wood or stone. Since prehistoric times this workmanship has not changed essentially, except that knife and chisel are now made of metal, while in the earliest periods they were of stone. Painting is done on paper, canvas, wood or plaster walls — all prepared first in a very complicated process — with artificial colors and the use of the most varied types of brushes. Such a practice cannot be imagined except in a civilization of highly developed cities, while sculpture can still be produced, if necessary, in the wildest forests or barren mountains, with instruments made by the sculptor himself.

The feeling for form is born in all of us; an understanding of painting is limited to a few. The child in grasping an object begins to develop unconsciously its plastic sense. If it uses a spoon, or later fork and knife, it holds a piece of plastic form in its hand, which if well formed has sculptural value. Sculpture, therefore, is connected with practical purposes, an understanding of it is constantly trained by both hand and eye. Painting is a purely ideal performance, without any practical use. An understanding of it depends mainly upon the training of the eye. Painting is further away from the necessities of life, its creation passes through a longer process of thinking than sculpture.

Relation of sculpture to human body

Every piece of sculpture, whether it represents human, animal or inorganic forms, is related to man inasmuch as, like man, it occupies a three-dimensional space. Painting is two-dimensional and, therefore, in its material substance unrelated to man. This relationship of sculpture to our person expresses itself first in size. Sculpture has a size which we are able to grasp. Either it is of the same size as man himself, or it may be somewhat larger or very much smaller, but man will always feel himself its equal, as if he were able to embrace it or take it into his hands. If the piece of sculpture is out of proportion to man, if it attempts to dominate or overpower him, it is seldom successful except in purely abstract forms of symbolic and religious content (obelisk, totem-pole, etc.). So great an age of sculpture as the Middle Ages did not have the so-called monumental sculpture of oversized human figures which have no relation to man. The vertical structures of the cathedrals were divided into storeys, each, with its decoration of sculptures, related to man's size. It is true that the Greeks and Romans practised the monumental, superhuman type of sculpture which developed out of the primitive symbolic sculpture, but it is perhaps fortunate that the few realistic statues of enormous size, of the fifth century and of later epochs, have not been preserved for us. In general, the works of classical times were of human size.

But it is not size alone, it is the lifelike quality inherent in a good piece of sculpture, which brings us near to it. If we encounter such a work, it intrigues us because in its appearance there is something similar to ourselves. It is as if we were to meet a ghost that had taken on some of our own qualities: it is not a human or other being, yet it seems alive and produces in us a feeling of close spiritual kinship, such as no painting can awaken in us. The primitive man when he sees a realistic sculpture may actually think at first that it is alive. After he has found that this is not so, he gives the work a symbolic name, which means that he believes it to be related to him, although the body of the sculpture is of a different substance from his own.

Inasmuch as sculpture has volume, it is more like architecture than painting. Architecture, however, covers volume, like a shell which we can see from outside and from inside. It is just like sculpture in regard to proportions related to man. But sculpture can never become as much a part of us as architecture can, for we see it only from the outside, although in its limited scope, its narrow circumference, it is more like our own body.

It is probably on account of this relation to our own body that we like sculpture only if it expresses volume, since we unconsciously conceive ourselves as volume. If the volume is dissolved, we feel comfortable only if the empty space thus created can be easily filled in by imagination and, embraced by the remaining solid part, forms the supplementary section to a well-rounded whole. Sculptures with partly open spaces can be compared to the human body with partly outstretched legs or arms; they may be stretched out to a certain distance, providing empty spaces in between, but we always feel that these spaces form part of a whole and that they do not overstep the limits set by the body's circumference.

6

However, as we shall see later, there exists a type of dissolved sculpture which satisfies our imagination, even if it goes beyond the limits set by the idea of a well-balanced whole, that is, if the sculpture expresses rapid movement. If man or animal is running, or if an inorganic element like water or a mechanical object like an engine or a plane is in rapid movement, their volume seems to dissolve completely. But it only seems so; in reality, the solid mass of which the moving object exists does not change. Thus, if this dissolving created by strong motion is expressed in sculpture, the outlines of the sculpture may well be broken through in one or in several directions, entirely changing the shape of the object, but the composition will not appear convincing if the sculpture has not at the same time the solidity and the connection with the earth which the human, or any other body known to our experience, actually has.

Since sculpture is so closely related to the human body, being as it were a repetition of its weight in some form, which painting is not, it took precedence over painting in the development of the arts. It is true that we know of prehistoric cave paintings, but it can hardly be doubted that, on account of their sophisticated style, they are the product of a comparatively late civilization which was preceded by earlier, more primitive ones. The earliest works of art are works of sculpture, ranging from stone implements to stone effigies of symbolic character. The importance attached to sculpture by early peoples is proved by the fact that in the earliest historical periods, from those of the Babylonians and Egyptians on through those of the Greeks, Romans and the art-producing nations of the Middle Ages, sculpture was the leading art. Only in recent times, since the fifteenth century, has painting become predominant.

Chapter II

Appeal to the Sense of Touch

*Importance of
sculpture in primitive
periods*

One can touch a piece of sculpture as if it were an organic being; it reminds one of organic forms. There is no sensation in touching a painting. It is true that painting can give the illusion of nature more effectively than sculpture, but to primitive man the reality of actual volume in sculpture is particularly significant, because his emotions are more developed than his intellect. To civilized man also, the direct connection with organic form which sculpture provides never loses its appeal, for art and sensuality are closely related.

The earliest art we know, that of the paleolithic period, is plastic art. The beautifully cut stone implements of this epoch, and of the neolithic age, appeal at least as much to the sense of touch as they do to the eye (Fig. 8). The stone hammers and knives are indeed visually pleasing in outline and form, but we cannot understand their artistic value if we see them only exhibited in cases. We have to take them into our hands and feel their pleasant smoothness; they are made to fit the hand. It was this warmth of touch which the earliest stone sculptor sought; in it he unconsciously recognized the superiority of sculpture over painting. The same generalization applies to early pottery. The best pieces of pre-Columbian, Peruvian and Central American ceramics, for instance, have to be handled if we want to understand the remarkable sensitiveness of their makers in modeling the surfaces.

Good sculpture develops the sense of touch. And it is not always necessary to touch it; it is sufficient to know that one can do so. A sculpture has no value if it does not awaken in us this longing.

*Pleasure in
touching sculpture*

How closely art is connected with the sense of touch can be easily observed in museums, where uneducated visitors often can hardly be prevented from handling the objects. The educated, too, sometimes have such desires: a visitor once told me that only with the greatest self-control could she restrain her fingers when enamoured of a beautiful painting. If such visitors actually touch the paintings, they are very much disillusioned, for there is nothing in the object to which they can react; but they obtain what they long for, at least to some degree, if they touch a piece of sculpture. Sculpture can give a great deal of pleasure to the blind, as we learn from the visit Helen Keller paid to certain sculptors' studios; painting, of course, cannot give the blind this pleasure.

Children are especially fond of fingering sculpture if the subject appeals to their imaginations. In the Detroit Museum there is a piece of bronze sculpture by Renée Sintenis, representing a young donkey in

11

about half-size. The mouth, ears and back of the animal have been so rubbed by children's hands that the gold-colored metal now shines through the black patina, resulting in a very pleasing effect. It is well known that various sacred statues in Roman churches have been touched or kissed so often that those portions which could be reached by the worshiper have had to be covered with protecting metal.

Patina
caused by handling

Sculptures are not always damaged by being touched a great deal. Indeed, certain kinds have their surface appearance improved by frequent rubbing; such, for instance, is the case with African Negro carvings and Renaissance bronzes. The beautiful, enamel-like black tone of some of the finest African sculptures is due to frequent handling, and the shiny, golden-brown surface of some Renaissance bronze statuettes is not the result of an artificial patina but of the handling of many generations. As with certain prehistoric implements, the quality of these sculptures cannot be completely understood unless their forms are felt by the fingers.

While artists have frequently observed that sculptures of the Renaissance and of the classical period can be completely understood in their beauty only if caressed by the hand, it is less generally known that this applies also to mediaeval plastic art. A large Italian crucifix of the thirteenth century, carved in wood, in the Detroit Museum (Figs. 9, 10), which because of its simplified forms and imposing outlines had been placed high so as to be seen from a distance, revealed to the fingers, when studied at close range, marvelous details of structure, for instance, of the collar-bones and of the veins in the hands and feet, which otherwise can hardly be seen even in strong light. It is obvious that the vibrating effect of the surfaces is greatly due to workmanship based upon a precise study of nature and yet subordinated (a characteristic of the period) to abstract forms.

Early marble sculptures, too, often show — and not always to their disadvantage — the consequences of the public's irresistible desire to handle them. Let us take as an example the beautiful tombs of members of the royal family of the Valois, in Naples churches, by the great Italian Gothic sculptor, Tino di Camaino, which are usually supported by statues of Virtues. One would suppose that spectators would have been satisfied by looking admiringly at the figures, without placing fingers upon them. But the statues within reach of the visitors have been touched so frequently through the centuries that their surface has become ivory-colored, brownish and shiny (Fig. 11), while those higher up have the white and dull tone of the original marble (Fig. 12). The difference is so great that some critics have thought two different sculptors were responsible.

Relation of
children and women
to plastic art

The pleasure that primitive people and children receive in touching the plastic form is expressed in their fondness for dolls and toys of human or animal shape, without which their enjoyment of life could not be imagined. Even the most animated colored drawing cannot give a child the feeling of real life as much as its doll or teddy-bear can. It is well known that girls are more susceptible to toys of plastic form than boys, obviously because their imaginations from an early age are preoccupied by motherly instincts. For this reason, women often have a better understanding of sculpture than men. It is also not accidental that we have had so many women sculptors in recent times. To do plastic work seems to be natural to woman, who, compared with man, has more facility with her fingers. On the other hand, she seems to have greater difficulty in giving style to her work, while man works with clearer, more logical perceptions. If we do not know of many sculptresses in early periods, it is because only the emancipation of women in modern times has given them opportunity of using their talent.

The great sculptors could not develop in us the strong appeal of the tactile sense if they did not themselves possess the emotional and sensual qualities necessary to produce such effects. If we read the biographies of well-known sculptors, it is easy to find evidence of these traits, and I may mention some remarks of Rodin, Maillol and Brancusi, related by their friends.

Gsell, in his book on Rodin, reports the following episode:[1] One evening Rodin showed him a small antique torso of the Venus of Medici and held a lamp up to it. "Is it not wonderful?" Rodin cried. "Confess you did not expect to discover so much detail! Just look at the numberless undulations of the hollow which unites the body to the thigh. Notice all the voluptuous curvings of the hip. And now, here, the adorable dimples along the loins." He spoke in a low voice, with devout ardor, bending over the marble as if he loved it. "It is truly flesh," he said. And beaming, he added, "You would think it moulded by kisses and caresses." Then, suddenly laying his hand on the statue, "You almost expect when you touch the body to find it warm."

When Maillol went with his friends to the Acropolis in Athens for the first time, one of the guards with difficulty prevented him from climbing upon the Erechtheion, where he wished to embrace one of the magnificent Caryatids whose beauty moved and intoxicated him. He used to caress the ancient stones with an almost religious love, while he medi-

1. Auguste Rodin, *Art;* 1912, p. 55.

tated on the classical masters who seemed so close to him beneath the skies of Greece.[2]

Of Brancusi, Malvina Hoffman relates the following remark: "Sculpture must be lovely to touch, friendly to live with, not only well made."[3] One of the masterpieces of Brancusi is his egg-shaped composition, *Sculpture pour les aveugles* (Fig. 13), the title of which sufficiently expresses the artist's desire to give through his piece of sculpture as much pleasure to the touching hand as to the eye. In this connection it may be mentioned that Marcel Duchamp, one of the initiators of the modern movement, experimented with a kind of sculpture created purely to touch, not to see; he enclosed the form in a box with an opening at the top large enough to allow passage of the hand, which could move over the form within.

We do not need to touch a piece of sculpture like the *Human Concretion* by the Swiss sculptor Hans Arp (Fig. 14), we can caress it with our senses, even in a photographic reproduction. It affects us as beautifully shaped pebbles on some beaches do, but it has an additional aesthetic value given it by a conscious artist's mind, a symbolism expressed in a carefully thought-out composition, while the pebbles have only accidental forms.

We observe that imagination carries the artist confronted with the sculpture he loves as far as it carries the child who treats its doll as if it were alive. This fact reveals furthermore how closely the awareness of plastic volume is connected in the sculptor's mind with his sensuousness.

Sensuousness in prehistoric and modern sculpture balanced by cosmic tendencies

Like the child, primitive man is remarkably frank of expression in this respect. The earliest plastic figures known to us — executed, perhaps, 20,000 to 15,000 B.C. — are astonishing in their representation of voluptuous female figures: the famous so-called Venus of Willendorf (Fig. 15), the ivory statuettes from Brassempuy and Lespuque (Fig. 16). At the same time these figures are executed with a sure instinct for expression in plastic value. They are conceived as cubic volumes, abstract in outline, balanced in height and breadth; the forms develop into space on all sides. The volume is penetrated by planes which shift through one another and give us the impression of seeing the inside and the outside simultaneously — all problems which our time has taken up again after so many centuries and which in these examples were solved with the greatest ease by men who stood at the dawn of history.

Not long ago these works of prehistoric sculpture were considered un-

2. John Rewald, *Maillol;* 1939, p. 17.
3. Malvina Hoffman, *Sculpture Inside and Out;* 1938, p. 53.

worthy of an art museum and of merely archaeological interest. The questionable theories of nineteenth-century historians, according to which art improved slowly from a beginning in earliest periods to the perfected works of classical times, blinded the eyes to these remarkable accomplishments at mankind's very start. Since we know that the highest creative work bursts into reality with full force and perfection, like all newly born creatures, one might say, with equal reason, that art was greatest at its commencement and afterwards slowly declined. The correct conception, however, probably lies between these two theories. After great beginnings, a decline ensues, until suddenly a new creation of extraordinary force starts a new period of production. Certainly the earliest plastic work of human hands can be as little surpassed in artistic value as the animal paintings of paleolithic cave-dwellers, which have found more favor with the art-loving public.

What is astonishing is that, perhaps for the first time in history, we are today able to understand to the full the artistic intentions of remotest prehistoric man, whose emotions, in no way hampered by intellectual considerations, must have been of an unheard-of intensity. This fact alone should prove that we are living in times during which the emotions are of a somewhat similar intensity — times during which, in art, purely intellectual values have little place.

It is not difficult to find outstanding sculpture executed in our day in which these emotional, sensuous qualities are as pronounced as in the earliest prehistoric sculpture or in certain images among primitive African and Polynesian tribes. As an example, we reproduce one of the most important bronzes by Gaston Lachaise, his floating figure (Fig. 17). The proportions are what we normally call Michelangelesque; that is, while the figure is not more than life-size the individual parts are exaggerated enormously — and subordination of the head in relation to the body, in size and expression, was, as we have noticed, anticipated in Michelangelo's works. Yet the essentials of the figure are much nearer to the conception of the prehistoric statuette of Lespuque. The outlines are reduced to almost geometric curves; the forms are simplified to such a degree that the piece fits perfectly into an ellipsoid. This ellipsoid is placed sideways, in the case of Lachaise's sculpture, but whether it floats or stands upright in space like the prehistoric figure is unessential. The main point is that this figure is no longer realistically grounded upon the earth like Michelangelo's figure, but exists by itself, free of the earth, in an indefinite space.

That this is not an isolated example in modern art we shall see if we study the work of other modern sculptors; Flannagan, for instance, a very different personality from Lachaise, achieves the same degree of expression with similar results (Figs. 18, 19). His sculptures frequently run down to a narrow point in the center, contrary to the principles of Renaissance sculptures, which are solidly built up in the form of a pyramid. Flannagan's creatures are hardly connected with the earth at all; they swell in the center like a balloon that rises from the ground.

The connection of original modern sculpture with prehistoric and primitive art, the similarity in their expression of unconscious emotions, proves clearly, if nothing else, that we are in the midst of the birth of a new era in art which is opposed to that of the preceding centuries and which harks back to ideas of ages far beyond the horizon.

We have not sufficient historical knowledge of how people reacted when such a cleavage between two eras occurred long ago, for instance at the end of archaic art in Greece, or at the beginning of mediaeval art. We have knowledge of this reaction in only one case nearer to us in history, when the Renaissance movement revealed itself, in other words, when that art was introduced which is now opposed by artists. Then people suddenly came to the conviction that they were allied to an epoch long past, to classical antiquity, and that all that had been produced during the interval — Romanesque and Gothic art — was of little value. Later centuries have discovered that the difference between Renaissance and classical art was greater than people believed at that time and that Renaissance art was as original as classical art. From this parallel, we may conclude that modern art which is related to the earliest art is not a repetition or imitation, but is an original creation, produced out of similar elementary emotions, which have been stimulated by the discovery of these spiritually related products of a past age.

1. *M. Le Nain, Painter's Studio*

2. *H. Robert, Sculptor's Studio*

3. *Leonardo da Vinci*
4. *Michelangelo*

5. *Leonardo da Vinci*
6 and 7. *Michelangelo*

8. *Prehistoric Implements*

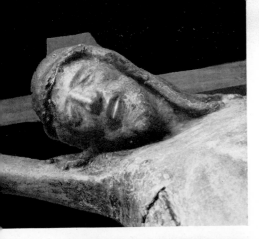

10. *Detail of Figure 9*

11 and 12. *Tino di Camaino*

9. *Italian, 13th century*

13. *C. Brancusi*

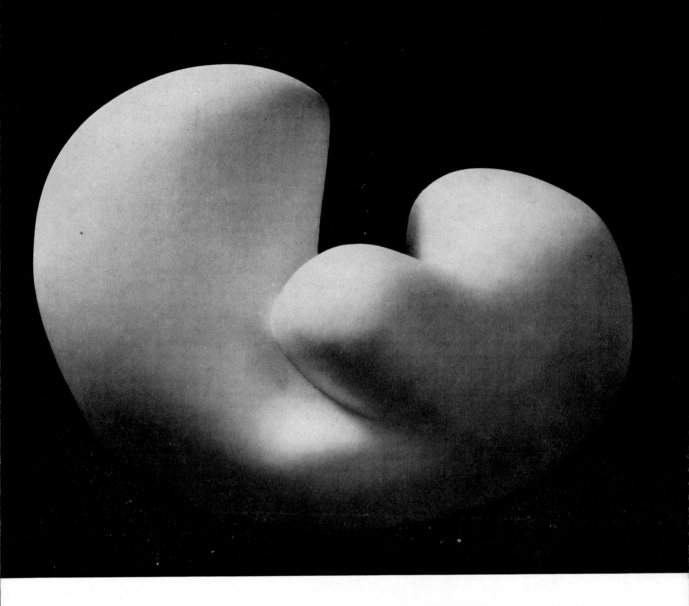

14. *H. Arp*
15. *Prehistoric*

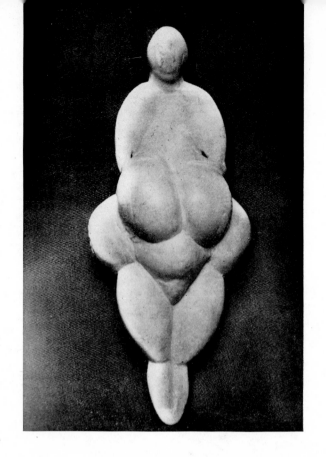

16. *Prehistoric*

17. *G. Lachaise*

Chapter III

Means of Creating the Appearance of Life

Necessity of accentuation so as to create life

Sculpture, like all art, desires to create life. To this the material from which sculpture is made is opposed, because its original function was a different one. Whether it be bronze, stone or wood, every material has a life of its own, even if merely the life of an inorganic part of nature. The artist, therefore, in using this material for his purposes needs enormous vitality in order to be able to conquer and to penetrate its opposing strength with his own. We do not believe in what the artist creates if it does not radiate life in every part. The greater the artist, the greater will be the over-abundance of energy which he communicates to the apparently dead material, whose innate life qualities he must turn to his own ends. It is a mistake to think that the life comes from the material or from the model: it comes only from the maker.

How is the dynamic force of the sculptor used so as to convince us that his work is alive? He cannot, like nature, work from within by making a body grow with the help of cells, blood-vessels, muscles, nerves; he can work only on the outside of the material he employs. He must therefore substitute other means to make us believe in the real existence of his creation. He can do this only by *exaggerating* and *accentuating* certain elements in his sculptures, which will appear to the spectator as the most life-creating parts.

That the painter uses exaggeration to produce effects equivalent to those of nature is well known. If, for instance, he wants to paint sunlight, he must exaggerate the contrasts of light and shadow, or compose the light out of a heightened intensity of the primary colors of the spectrum, which, when mixed by the spectator's eye, produce a greater luminosity than if mixed upon the palette. But that the sculptor has to work towards similar ends is often not realized, especially by those amateurs who attempt to copy a fragment of nature exactly and then find that their work lacks vitality and composition.

Danger in casting from life

The sculptor who makes plastic forms with his own hands is nearer the earth than the painter, hence is in great danger of copying nature directly by casting its forms. That sculpture can be created by this copying method is a very old misconception. We may read in Vasari that Verrocchio invented the method of making life masks in plaster, which were used for realistically painted portrait busts, and that many Florentine families ordered busts of this kind from his studio. Another artist of Verrocchio's time, Orsino, executed similar busts in wax. Although these wax busts have disappeared — and we do not regret it — we can still judge how the painted plaster or terracotta busts of the Florentine Renaissance, made with the help of life or death masks, looked. Some, like that in the Detroit Museum (Fig. 20), were made by able artists who expertly added the rest of the head, the bust and upper arm. But in spite of the skill employed, the composition appears to be disjointed and the expression has in it something unpleasant and mean. The life mask preserves the minutest details of the skin, but nothing of the life beneath it. Even in cases where the artist remodeled the forms, usually distorted around the mouth, and added the pupils in a correct manner, he was not able to imbue these empty forms with much of the spirit.

The naive and uneducated spectator is easily deceived by the outward likeness of the features. Thus it happened that when sculpture started to develop in America in the earlier part of the nineteenth century, the mechanical art of life-mask portraiture had considerable success. Clark Mills (1815–1883), who executed the first bronze equestrian statue in this country, that of General Jackson (in Washington), started his career by "taking casts from the living face which enabled him to make portrait busts so cheaply that he soon had as much work as he could do" (Lorado Taft).

Busts done from life masks by another American sculptor — should we call him sculptor? — John H. I. Browere, have been recently discovered and exhibited (Figs. 21, 22). Indeed, if modern photography is cleverly applied to them, as was done by the publishers, they produce a remarkably realistic, almost surrealistic, effect; but considered in themselves they are the opposite of good sculpture. It has been said that Browere showed himself a real artist in the additions he made to complete the busts, but we find that precisely the contrary is true. How inept an artist he was in this respect is shown by the fact that he tried to cast, not only the face, but everything, including ears, neck and bust, which was necessary to complete the bust of his model. We learn this from the diary of Thomas Jefferson, who gives a careful description of the procedure he had to endure when Browere made his life mask. After most of his upper garments had been removed, Jefferson tells us that "successive layers of thin grout" were applied by the artist to face, neck and chest. This operation took more than an hour, and the great man, who was eighty-two years of age and in ill health, almost suffocated. Though Jefferson endured the experience with good humor, his family was greatly concerned about it. When Browere wanted to take off the plaster, it had become so dry, Jefferson continues, "that separation became difficult and even dangerous. He was obliged to use freely the mallet and chisel to break it into pieces and get off a piece at a time. These strokes of the mallet would have been sensible almost to a loggerhead turtle. I was quite exhausted and there became real danger that the ears would tear from the head sooner than from the plaster. It was a dangerous experiment on his part." Only an inferior artist could make such blunders! And indeed Browere's portraits, although they are interesting historical documents, give an entirely distorted idea of the character of his sitters. Some undoubtedly great men — fortunately not Jefferson — are made to look as if they had come out of an insane asylum. They have nearly all that deadly meanness of expression which seems to be left in faces that lack spirituality.

The only people who seem to have been able to treat life masks in an artistic manner were the Egyptians. The best preserved were found in the studio of a sculptor of the Tel-Amarna period, Tutmose, who lived about 1370 B.C. (they are now in the Berlin Museum). But even these masks cannot be regarded as anything else than studies for this artist's finished works in stone. These casts, compared with the sculptor's own busts, show that a work of art can be produced only if it is penetrated throughout every part by the personality of the artist.

Often the great sculptor does not himself realize how much of his own personality and life power he infuses into his works. Rodin, among others, is a typical example. Gsell, while watching Rodin study from the life model, observed that the sculptor changed certain forms, accentuating here and there parts which gave expression to the movement of the figure. When Gsell remarked to Rodin that he was changing nature to accord with his own ideas, Rodin was annoyed and said that this was not true, that all he did was to copy nature. Similarly, when a young woman who was studying with the sculptor Kolbe asked how she might be able to imbue her works with more style, she was told, "It is quite sufficient if you imitate nature; if you do it faithfully, you will create good sculpture." Even so, there can be no doubt that Rodin as well as Kolbe unconsciously altered nature when they created.

Maillol said about his art, *"Je n'invente rien."* But at another time he remarked, contradicting himself, "Form pleases me and I make it, but for me it is a means of expressing an idea. I look for ideas. . . . That is why it is nothing to copy the nude. Reproducing a nude woman does not mean making a statue. . . ." This proves that great artists should not be taken too literally when they express theories about art. Those who are able to formulate such theories in a manner that furthers the understanding of art for the critical mind are often not the best artists. This is natural, because those who devote their time to trying to express in words what they should be expressing in forms are deviating from their original path, which a great artist would never do.

The first sculptor in recent times to question the assumption that imitation of nature by an accomplished sculptor results in artistic conception was Adolf Hildebrand, whose activity in Munich in the eighties of the nineteenth century started a new movement of simplified classicist style in German sculpture. He was of the opinion that the artist has to build up, out of the accidental and fragmentary elements in nature used for his composition, an harmonious construction of his own, which appears as lawful to the human eye as does nature as a whole. It is characteristic that in his essay, *Problems of the Figurative Arts,* Hildebrand is convincing, but that he is not as spontaneous and original a sculptor as those mentioned before.

Different possibilities of accentuation: Exaggeration of volume

The accentuation of those portions of the work of sculpture in which life expresses itself most intensely may proceed in different ways. For instance, the sculptor may exaggerate the volume of the individual parts of his figures: Michelangelo knew this better than anyone. His figures are seldom more than life-size, yet they appear enormous because certain parts of the body are increased to almost double the size they would have in reality. It would be impossible, for instance, to imagine as alive the reclining figures from the Medici tombs, yet the vitality produced by the swelling of their muscles and the increased volume of their limbs is so overpowering that we believe in their existence and never think of measuring them by the standard of ordinary human beings.

In modern art we find a parallel in Maillol's *Action in Chains* (Fig. 23), but more so in some of Lachaise's figures, his *Standing Woman* in the Whitney Museum and his *Standing Man* (Fig. 24) in the Museum of Modern Art. Without Michelangelo's precedent, they could not have been imagined, but they are essentially inspired by the ideas of our time and contain elements that can be understood only today.

The function of the accentuation of the body in Michelangelo's figures is to give immense strength for an all-round movement and twisting of the body. Spiritually the figures are shut up in themselves and do not communicate with the outer world. In Lachaise, the accentuations are the expression of a constant growth, which we witness at the moment of its sudden expansion. It is significant that the artist has been able to make us actually aware of the body's increase to enormous proportions in that moment. This expanding movement reaches into space in all directions. It expresses the longing of the human mind to extend towards the cosmos and reveals its ultimate ability to become one with that cosmos. In the female statue this same expansion appears as an unconscious élan, which fills the body with new and greater volume, at the same time lifting it up from the ground; in the man, the expansion is the result of an heroic resolution, expressing the will of the figure in a triumphant gesture of elation.

Exaggeration of functional parts of the body

Another factor in achieving the illusion of life in sculpture is evident in the work of the Renaissance sculptors from Donatello to Giovanni da Bologna, and most of all in the work of Michelangelo. By stressing to such a degree those parts of the human body where movement originates and functions — the neck muscles, the shoulder bones, the elbows and knees, the wrists and the ankles — we are at once made aware of their life (Fig. 4). Gothic sculptors were little interested in this kind of emphasis on individual sections of human structure; a continuous rhythm flowing through the bodies, connecting them with the lines of architecture, gave to their figures sufficient life-enhancing quality.

Exaggeration of movement

Another method of increasing the feeling of life in a piece of sculpture is by exaggeration of movement, although this does not necessarily mean extravagant movement of the body or the extremities. It may be sufficient that the figure makes only one small step forward, that the position of the lower forearm diverges slightly, as in Egyptian (Fig. 25) and early Greek sculptures. In the case of these figures, however, we see that the internal movement of the whole body is greatly exaggerated: every muscle in arms, legs and hips is strained to the utmost, so that we witness a tremendous effort forced upon the body by the forward step of the foot or the lifting of the arm.

In the advanced stage of realistic sculpture, when the limbs move freely in all directions, the motion of the body as represented in a good piece of sculpture is always greater than we should expect in real life under similar circumstances. This applies even to the most harmonious figures of the classical period of Greek art. Try to imitate the position of a statue like the *Diadoumenos,* the *Wounded Amazon* or the *Idolino,* of the time of Polycletus or Phidias, and you will find that the pose which seems so simple and natural is in reality very complicated and unnatural. The *Diadoumenos,* for instance, would probably be better able to fasten the band around his forehead if he were to stand still — not continue walking — while doing so.

Rodin, who was an excellent observer, explained that Greek statues — he was referring to those of the advanced period — have generally four directions of movement, counting from head to foot, these directions being alternately opposed to each other. This complicated system is increased in Rodin's own figures and in those of his predecessors in French art, like Rude, whom he admired. In the bronze statue of Marshal Ney by Rude, or in the *St. John the Baptist* by Rodin (Fig. 26), a transitional movement is selected in which the different directions of the upper and lower parts of the body are brought about by different, although closely consecutive actions of the will.

It is interesting to mention in this connection that when Rodin explained why the forward-striding movement of his St. John was so convincing and why it did not agree with a photograph of a walking figure (which seems to rest motionless on one leg or to hop on one foot), he again refuted the remark of Gsell to the effect that the great artist at times works contrary to nature. Rodin insisted that his work was truer to nature than the camera.

Contraposto movement

Here a word may be said about *contraposto,* which has always and rightly been considered a characteristic of Renaissance sculpture, and which, though especially in the time of Donatello and Michelangelo, was also employed in the seventeenth and eighteenth centuries in European art. This term indicates a corresponding movement of arms and legs in opposite directions, in such a manner that, for instance, when the left foot is placed backward, the right arm will be placed forward and the left arm backward (see Michelangelo's *Slave,* Fig. 4). A similar contraposto movement can be applied to groups of two or more figures.

To some degree, contraposto is a natural movement; in walking we use the opposite hands and feet in a crosswise, corresponding movement. When contraposto is used in sculpture, however, it is greatly exaggerated and systematized. If we tried to imitate these movements, we should find it quite strenuous to maintain the positions for any length of time. This proves again that the sculptor, in his endeavor to create life, has to exaggerate natural functions and impose upon them some kind of obvious law which can be grasped easily by the spectator.

The contraposto movement has been used not only by Renaissance sculptors for compositional purposes, but also by the Greek and Roman masters. We encounter it in many famous classical statues like the *Idolino,* the *Wounded Amazon,* the *Doryphoros* and so on; but here it is employed with less consistency than in the Renaissance and with less continual exaggeration in the twisting of the extremities. That contraposto was used by Gothic sculptors has not as yet been observed, so it seems, but there do exist French and German sculptures of the fourteenth century in which these formal ideas, which are generally thought to be known only to the Renaissance masters, are fully developed. For

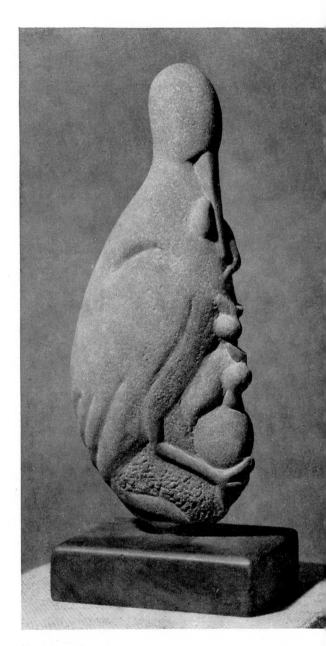

18. *J. B. Flannagan*   19. *J. B. Flannagan*

20. *Florentine, 15th century*

21. *J. H. I. Browere*

22. *J. H. I. Browere*

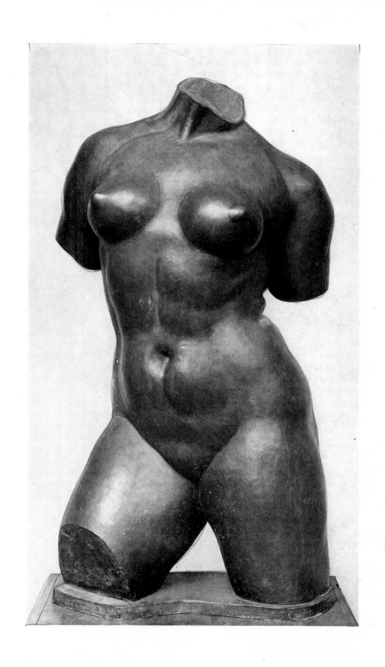

23. *A. Maillol*

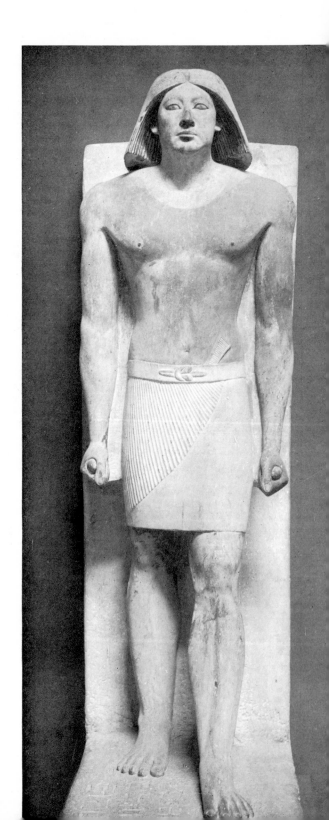

24. *G. Lachaise*

25. *Egyptian, 5th Dynasty*

26. *A. Rodin*

27. *Freiburg*

38

28. Ile-de-France, 14th century

29. *Etruscan, 6th century* B.C.
30. *Greek, 6th century* B.C.
31. *Etruscan, 6th century* B.C.

example, we reproduce two statues of holy kings from Freiburg Cathedral (Fig. 27) where the contraposto of the extremities is conspicuously and very successfully carried out within the compact silhouette of a sitting figure.

That Gothic sculptors also knew how to adapt these contraposto movements to whole groups can be seen in the exquisite rhythmic composition of a French fourteenth-century stone relief from the Ile-de-France in the Metropolitan Museum of Art (Fig. 28). The contrast between figures seen from the front and those seen from the back, between uplifted and lowered arms and correspondingly placed feet, is here as carefully employed as in the battle scenes in reliefs by the young Michelangelo or his master Bertoldo.

Nowadays we are less interested in these problems of Greek and Renaissance sculptures, or even in those of eighteenth- or nineteenth-century French works, as far as individual movement is concerned. That system of stressing movement is too complicated for our modern conception and is too much concerned with the importance of the individual, regardless of his connection with the cosmos. The over-estimation of the human being in comparison with other aspects of nature results in a representation of human force in terms of isolated, tortured and self-sufficient individuals, as we have seen in the art of Michelangelo and of Rodin.

Connecting the individual figure with the life-stream outside of it

In other periods, during which the relation to the cosmos is so strongly felt that individuality loses its value, the artist aims at exactly the opposite; he shows individual strength protracted to such a degree that the body appears devoid of all personal will power, which is replaced by an external energy that controls movement of itself (Figs. 29, 30, 31). In this case the sculptor works unconsciously with exaggeration and accentuation in order to make his point clear and, at the same time, to produce the appearance of vitality. Thus, we will sometimes find his figures stretched out to enormous length, their volume reduced, their muscular strength lacking and their loose and angular limbs acting like those of puppets moved by wires. Such tendencies can be observed in the paleolithic period, the primitive Greek and Etruscan periods and in certain phases of Gothic and modern art.

Outside life-stream felt in prehistoric, Gothic and modern art

Wherever we encounter this submersion of the individual, we may be certain that a strong mass movement forms the historical background, for the subconscious emotional elements in the culture of such epochs are stronger than in those of individualistic ages. The masses are ruled by a powerful belief that unites them spiritually, whether it be of the

41

cosmos, or of an earthly power in the form of a church, or a worldly ruler recognized as the spiritual guide.

This background of belief produces a state of mind which we imagine to have been felt in the earliest prehistoric period like an unconscious chain binding the as yet small groups of human beings together in adherence to the same cosmic force. The memory of this connection with the cosmos, from which mankind at some time originally sprang, was probably still alive in primitive subconsciousness to a degree unimaginable today.

Connection with mass movement in these periods

We know that the mass movement which united the Greeks as a people, and formed their national characteristics, took place from the tenth to the eighth century B.C., when they were ruled by democratic leaders of the army, elected by the people and representing their common belief in a superior, spiritual guiding force. A similar movement seems to have existed among the Etruscans during approximately the sixth century B.C. In both these epochs we find elongated types among the representations of God as well as of worshipers.

Examples in Greek and Etruscan art

Archaeologists, who only in recent times have recognized the importance of these figures, have given different explanations for their unusual style (Figs. 29, 30, 31). In the Apollo statuette in Boston (Fig. 30), Curtius believes the long neck, rich hair and large eyes to be attributes of a young god, characterizing his spiritual superiority. Buschor, in his penetrating studies, explains the elongated forms as an expression of the idea of growth. Indeed, if we look intently at this figure, it seems as if it were growing before our eyes, or as if shoulders and hips were widening and the head rising to an unusual height, while the wide-open eyes seem to express astonishment at the miracle. It radiates vitality like a straight, slender tree in spring.

In the bronze statuette of a worshiper (Fig. 31), we feel the stream of life from a world beyond the visible one, passing through its curved line, absorbing its volume, yet adding an indefinable spirituality which connects it with the superior being to whom it prays.

in Gothic art

It is curious that in Gothic times the sculptor often arrived at similar solutions, by which a powerful life-stream from outside curves and elongates the figures according to the sculptor's own rhythm (Figs. 32, 33, 34). It is well known that the vertical lines of an architecture directed towards a transcendental world penetrate the figures placed before the walls, and that this architecture is an expression of a movement of the masses whose positive belief in the mediaeval church furnished the ideas and the labor necessary for its construction. That the sculptured works of this vertical tendency were not necessarily part of the architecture itself (as in Figs. 32 and 34) is to be seen by studying certain fourteenth-century tomb-stones, placed in different parts of a church (Fig. 33).

in modern art

When we come to modern art, we encounter some impressive sculptures of a type similar to the Gothic, and others similar to the early Greek or Etruscan. It can hardly be doubted that the sculptors of both types were acquainted with their predecessors of earlier periods, but it can also not be doubted that they created original works of beauty of their own, which were possible only because a social movement of somewhat like character to that of past epochs encouraged these tendencies.

*Martini
and de Fiori*

Two modern sculptors who were influenced by early Etruscan art are the leading Italian sculptor Arturo Martini (Figs. 35, 36) and the German sculptor of Italian origin, Ernesto de Fiori, now living in Brazil (Fig. 37). In the works of both artists we find the unconscious angular movements of people who are guided solely by their emotions and who behave as in a dream, with curious directness. De Fiori's man (1914) seems actually walking in a dream, stretching his hands out towards an invisible force that leads him; while his crouching woman (1923) (Fig. 37) is built up in a rhythm of jerky accents, quite different from what we are wont to see in traditional female nudes with their sweet, flowing lines.

Martini's sitting figure of a man drinking from a water jar (Fig. 35) has, like all his works, a naive charm in its natural, awkward pose. The angularity of the limbs is curiously contrasted to the full and long cylindrical body, which should be compared with the female figure from Freiburg Cathedral (Fig. 34). A detail from his large impressive relief *La Giustizia Cooperativa,* in Milan, represents a group of the Prodigal Son and his family (Fig. 36). All the figures have long bodies, loose limbs and a far-distant look in their astonished eyes, which makes them kin.

The individuality in all these sculptures is of no significance compared to the general likeness of type and the resemblance of sentiment which binds them together. Here is obviously the spirit of a mass movement which, with its strong faith in a common cause, creates figures of similar emotional attitude.

"The revolution of the masses" unfolds itself usually in two directions, in a mechanical and in a spiritual shape. The mechanization of our time is caused by the machine, which is driven by the masses and produces for the masses. It influences not only the philosophy of life but also man's body. The mechanical man acting like a machine has often been presented to us in satirical drawings and films. But reality is not far removed from these representations, as we may observe if we look carefully at the gestures and expressions of people who have been working in factories, handling machinery all their lives. We like to speak of freedom; but wherever there is factory life, no freedom of body or mind is possible. The workman who stands all day on the assembly-line becomes something of an automaton and reflects in his body the mechanical movements he is engaged in all day. His gestures will be jerky and angular, expressing his half-awake state of mind; they will not be easy and flowing as those of the few who can arrange life of their own free will. Military discipline is another product of mass movement and, though generally of short duration, it may result in an influence upon the individual similar to that of factory life. We often read in war bulletins of the soldier at the front, who during march or battle is so over-tired that his mind ceases to function, that he acts and moves as in sleep, without will power of his own. He behaves then according to a subconscious memory of the commands he is supposed to obey. Many soldiers when back in civilian clothes will never lose the mechanical style of movement they have had to learn in the army. It is probably not a coincidence that most of the Etruscan bronze figures with mechanically moving, angular limbs are those of warriors (Fig. 29).

While the motifs of some modern sculpture suggest only the mechanical forces produced by mass movement, most of them contain as well some expression of its ideal aspect. The ideals, although they may often seem distorted from our narrow point of view, are certainly not less lofty than those of the Middle Ages, for no great movement in history is possible without a strong emotional belief in the righteousness of its source.

Lehmbruck

In the sculptures of Lehmbruck (Figs. 38, 39) we see these ideals of the social revolution of our time expressed with the same high-mindedness as in the Gothic cathedral sculptures which impressed him during his stay in Paris. We feel at once that here is the product of a mass feeling, not of an individual; and although these sculptures are conceived independently of an architectural background, they are in themselves constructed like a piece of architecture. There is something left in them of the mechanization of modern movement; their limbs are much looser, their gestures more detached from the body than those of the statues of the Gothic period. The spirit within, however, is clearly directed towards a transcendental aim, as we see in the dreamlike yet severe expression of the faces of such figures as the *Rising Youth* (1913) and the *Kneeling Woman* (1911). The first is the figure of an ascetic whose mind is filled with profound philosophical thought (Fig. 39); the elongated legs and arms, which move as if attached by wires, stress the vertical tendency, and

44

32. *Nürnberg, 14th century*

33. *Würzburg, 14th century*

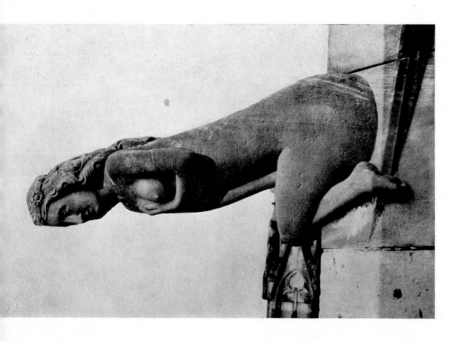

34. *Freiburg, 14th century*
35. *A. Martini*

46

36. *A. Martini*   37. *E. de Fiori*

38 and 39. *W. Lehmbruck*

39 a and 39 b. *C. Despiau*

40. *Indian, 12th century*

41. *N. Pisano*

42. *Donatello*

43. *Michelangelo*

44. *Agostino di Giovanni, 14th century*
45. *H. Gaudier-Brzeska*
46. *R. Duchamp-Villon*

47. *Negro Mask, Congo*
48. *Negro Idol, Congo*
49. *Negro Idol, Congo*

50. *Easter Island*
51. *Negro Sculpture, Gabun*
52. *Augsburg, 14th century*

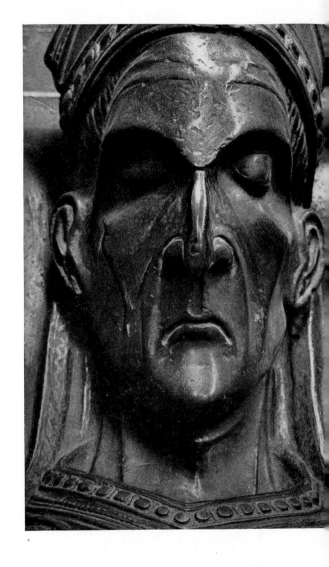

53. *Greek, c. 2500* B.C.

54. *Chinese, 7th century* B.C.

55. *H. Gaudier-Brzeska*

56. *G. Kolbe*

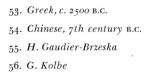

57. E. Barlach

58. *Venetian, 11th century*

59. *Tino di Camaino*

so does the head with high forehead, while the fingers of the right hand pointing to heaven indicate the direction of his ideas.

We feel this spirituality still more in the other figure (Fig. 38), whose long limbs are covered with a soft, flowing drapery, continued by the beautiful, swinging curves of the upper body and arms. This figure is carried away by a deep longing to ascend, but with an added modern touch of romantic melancholy. At the same time, the idea of growth is as obvious as in some of the early Greek figures. It is as if we were witnessing the slow opening of a flower, hesitating at the last moment, in shyness, before it unfolds into full bloom.

Despiau

The connection of modern sculpture with the mass movements of our time makes the existence of an art of individual portraiture precarious. Portraits like those by Gaudier-Brzeska and Duchamp-Villon (Figs. 45, 46) which, as we shall see in the next chapter, were inspired by religious images of primitive races, can hardly be called portraits of individuals. ("Do not expect that there will be much of you in it," said Gaudier when he modeled Pound's features.) Despiau is almost the only sculptor who is able to combine successfully in his portrait busts personal traits with characteristics expressing the common ideas of our epoch, although in the limited scope of a lyrical romanticism (Fig. 39a, b). But he belongs like Maillol to the older group of romantic classicists, who formed a reaction against Rodin and who are opposed to the modern movement. Yet he is one of the few accomplished sculptors of our time, and he is modern inasmuch as he goes far in drawing out general from individual traits and to such a degree that later generations may ask the question we are accustomed to ask in front of representations of mediaeval kings and emperors: Were the people of this period really so much alike, or did the contemporary demand for a unifying conception force the artist to overlook the individuality of his models?

Use of light and color

There are two other elements employed by the sculptor to give his work the semblance of life: light and color. Sculptures even more than paintings are dependent upon correct lighting. A fine piece of sculpture may, under poor light, lose all its plastic values and appear empty and expressionless, but, when lighted by the rays of the sun, suddenly come to life, because these plastic values are brought out by increasing the contrasts of light and shadow. The sunlight actually penetrates the pores of the stone; it produces shimmering reflections on the surface of bronze; it reveals the character of the wood in a piece of wood sculpture by striking the ridges of the grain; it thus creates lifelike qualities in the same

61

way that it gives life, by refreshing and reviving, to the human flesh and body. Naturally it is the sculptor who has prepared the surface of the material to receive this vital tonic when struck by the sun or even by artificial light. He has modeled the forms under conditions that favor strong contrasts of light and shadow, either out of doors in a warm climate, where the plastic forms are precisely defined under a clear sky, or indoors under properly directed artificial light. Nor can his work produce the wished-for effect unless it is seen under conditions of light similar to those in which it was conceived.

It has been said that sculpture should be produced and viewed only out of doors, but that would limit this particular art to southern countries and, even there, to special kinds of sculpture. However, we find that even in early times sculptors worked with artificial light when necessary. Vasari tells us of his visit to Michelangelo in the evening, when he found the artist chiseling marble by the light of a candle attached to his forehead. Artificial light is advantageous in that it can be brought so near to the sculpture that more of the modeling of the surface can be seen than in daylight. A sculptor will often show details of his work to someone visiting his studio by lighting a match or using a flashlight. For the same reason, it is justifiable to light sculptures in museums with artificial light, but at the same time opportunity should be given to see them under daylight.

As may be seen in Egypt and in India, sculptors discovered early in history that sunlight conveyed in channels from above or from the sides upon sculptures, increased the lifelike qualities. At Karnak, Egyptian temples were lighted by narrow slits placed high up on both sides of the nave. The statues inside received, in addition, dim light from the entrance door or, in sanctuaries, were lighted by a hole in the ceiling through which the rays fell directly upon the head of the statue. How strange an effect was created by this channeled lighting can still be observed in the sanctuary at Thebes.[1] In the Indian and Chinese temples built into rocks, the statues of Buddha are often lighted by rays of sunlight that fall upon them from openings in the front, the sides or the ceiling of the caves (Fig. 40). By these mysteriously entering light sources, the transcendental expression of the statues is increased.

The dim light of mediaeval churches forced the sculptor to exaggerate the contrasts of light and shadow in his statues by marking clearly the bone structure of faces and hands and by deeply undercutting the folds

1. For this information, I have to thank Mr. Ambrose Lansing, curator at the Metropolitan Museum of Art.

of costumes. For the same reason, many wood carvings and also some stone figures are realistically painted, even in those parts representing flesh. Hence, the colors may appear garish and exaggeratedly naturalistic if seen in the strong light of modern museums. It should, however, be considered that the strong color-realism of certain Gothic statues is always balanced by the abstract quality of their construction, which follows closely the style of architecture.

The mediaeval sculptor had a fine sense of the limits to which he could go without copying nature too obviously. When, for instance, the flesh parts are treated realistically with color, we may be sure that the tone of the costumes is of an unreal character, or that a strong application of gold, in draperies, nimbus or background will offset these naturalistic effects. The result will be in harmony with the other decorative furnishings in Gothic churches, such as stained glass windows, tapestries and so on, and will produce a transcendental and mystical effect in spite of certain realistic elements, whose additions were necessary for the purpose of expressing an intensified life.

Justification of color   We have come to the point where we may ask whether the addition of color is justified in marble sculpture. The material used for sculpture — stone, bronze, wood and clay — is almost monochrome when prepared for the hand of the sculptor. This is due to a mechanical process which cleans the surface, in the case of marble and wood, or purifies its substance, in the case of clay and bronze. Originally, these materials had a more colorful appearance, for nature does not permit a tiresome, monotonous and colorless exterior in any organic or inorganic objects on earth. It is a matter of course, therefore, that the sculptor should add color to these naked materials if he wants to give his work life. The question concerns merely how far he may proceed without becoming a copier of nature.

The reason why our time resents the otherwise useful collection of casts in museums, of which the former generation was so proud, is that their uniform grayish-white appears to us deadly and contrary to what we call lifelike. The idea of life in nature is to us, first of all, expressed by color. A wintry day with cloud-covered sky is deadliness itself, not so much because nothing seems to be growing — this is an afterthought on the part of the observer — but because without color nature is not alive for us. The moment the sun comes out, the colors begin to show, even in wintertime.

> — Aber die Sonne duldet kein Weisses
> Alles will sie mit Farbe beleben,

as Goethe says in *Faust*. But real life is not there until spring comes, when the colors are vivid and neutral gray has almost completely disappeared.

*Color in
Greek sculptures*

The Greeks were well aware of this and were not satisfied with the absence of color in large marble groups. It was a great surprise to archaeologists when, about thirty years ago, it was discovered that the temple sculpture in Greece had originally been colored. And with what colors! — not at all of a kind that scholars had expected in accordance with their conception of the advanced realism of the sixth and fifth centuries. The seemingly arbitrary colors contradicted their assumption of constant progress in the realistic treatment of forms. The early sculptures of the Acropolis were painted in large areas here and there with glowing, evenly applied, shadowless color planes; for instance, the bodies of horses and bulls were of a strong blue, the eyes of human figures vivid green, their hair blue: there seemed to be no relation to nature. Even at the end of the archaic period, the colors of marble groups, though less intense, possessed this unreal character; the horses' manes were painted blue, the hair and the eyes of human figures red.[2] Students explained to us that Greek sculptors in their color applications followed a purely decorative pattern, without considering the realism of the sculptural forms. This is only partly true.

Archaic Greek sculpture is not a step towards a developing realism in art, but is a highly developed and refined conventionalized style. And the color that was added to these forms had the same abstract quality. The sculptors discovered that the original tone of the beautiful Greek marble, with its glittering surface and golden, ivory-like shades, was sufficiently suggestive of reality as far as the flesh of the figures was concerned. But since the large expanse of marble in temple pediments and in other architectural parts with sculptural decorations would have looked monotonous without color, the sculptors added patches of strong color to certain places where the flesh was covered, such as draperies, animal skin, hair and ornaments. The colors, although decorative in themselves, moreover intensified the exalted character of these religious compositions and expressed a mood in accordance with the idealized forms. It is significant that blue, with its transcendental quality, and deep red, which reveals a glowing and fiery sentiment — both necessary for religious rapture — prevail in the color harmonies of these groups.

*Color in mediaeval
and Renaissance
sculpture*

We find the same tendency in mediaeval and Renaissance sculptors whose color applications we can judge with greater precision, since their works retain more traces than those of the early Greek sculptors. We

2. A. von Salis, *Die Kunst der Griechen;* 1922, p. 61.

observe that the flesh parts in marble sculptures are never painted, but that strong colors, primarily dark blue and gold, are used for hair and draperies. For instance, Nino Pisano (Fig. 41), one of the great Italian marble sculptors of the fourteenth century, employs only these two colors in his Madonna statues, gold for the hair of the Madonna and child, blue for the lining of her garments; otherwise the marble shows its original color. Both these colors (*azurro* and *oro*) were rare and very costly in this period; that they were used indicates that no expense was spared in adorning the images of the most holy figures. But there was a deeper significance: these two colors were symbolic of heaven; blue is the color of the sky during day, gold expressive of stars at night. Thus we find that colors, while suggestive of nature, have in Gothic art a higher, an ideal meaning when used in connection with religious representation.

These conceptions were adopted by Renaissance sculptors. Although the characteristic material used by the della Robbias was not marble, their problem of applying color to the white glazed ware was related to that of the marble sculptor. We shall consider here only the work of the two great masters of this form of sculpture, Luca della Robbia and his nephew Andrea, for the taste in the workshops that copied these leaders soon deteriorated. With our contemporary interest in an abstract style in sculpture, people are inclined to overlook the value of the art of the della Robbias, whose style is considered too realistic. But is this correct? It is true that the della Robbia forms are very close to nature, but the colors are not and they are applied in a manner that counterbalances the realism of the forms. The flesh parts are completely white, the eyes violet and the hair gilt. The only color like nature's is the blue of the background, which reminds us of the blue of the Italian sky. This color has the same symbolic meaning as in Greek and mediaeval sculptures; it corresponds to what is transcendental in the religious compositions.

Thus we find that, in the great epochs of the past, color is applied to sculpture, not in a meaningless, direct imitation of nature, but with the intention of increasing the lifelike quality of the work by intensifying its spiritual value.

Chapter IV

Planes

When speaking here of planes in sculpture, we mean clear-cut surfaces hewn into the block of which the piece of sculpture consists. But this is not the only meaning of "planes," used in connection with sculpture. We may, for instance, speak of relief planes and thereby refer to a relationship of the relief to the architecture which it adorns: such relief planes will be discussed in the next chapter. We also use the term "planes" in connection with abstract sculpture and in this case we mean sections into which the space has been divided. Because of the abstract nature of these planes, they may be imagined as shifting in different directions, as overcutting or interpenetrating and thus creating the illusion of an infinite space. Gaudier-Brzeska remarked that sculpture does not lend itself quite as well to the use of these shifting planes as painting does. This young French sculptor died in the first World War and, in expressing this opinion, he had in mind the heavy, untransparent material generally used for sculpture, like stone, bronze and wood. Since that time, certain thin or translucid materials, like sheets of metal, glass, plastics and so on, have been successfully adapted to the producing of plastic works; they allow the employment of shifting and interweaving planes to a degree almost as effective as in designs or paintings on flat surfaces.

But here we shall discuss planes in a much more limited sense, as applied to sculpture of human or other organic forms in stone, bronze, wood and clay, which are cut or modeled in such a manner that the characteristic traits of the object represented are brought out more clearly through these "planes." This use of planes is another means of creating the appearance of life by means of exaggeration and, as such, might have been discussed in the last chapter, but we prefer to deal with it in a special section, since the sculptures to which this method applies are vast in number. To these belong nearly all sculpture of the African Negroes and other primitive tribes, of most prehistoric and mediaeval peoples and of many contemporary artists. We might almost say that nowadays we cannot imagine a good piece of sculpture without clear-cut planes.

We should, however, remember that not all periods are marked by this preference for accentuated surface planes. The sculpture of the last five centuries did not stress them as much as the period before, but it is true that the conception of these epochs nearer to us is not the most appealing to our time. We are particularly fond of Donatello's and Michelangelo's unfinished sculptures, because, more than the finished ones, they reveal planes clearly; and this proves that even the great Renaissance masters —

and the same may be said of those of the Baroque — felt the necessity of working in planes, at least when the sculpture was in a preliminary state. A detail from Donatello's *David Martelli,* in the National Gallery in Washington, showing the right arm, and the upper part of the *Rondanini Pietà,* Michelangelo's last work, will make this point clear (Figs. 42, 43).

Undoubtedly the satisfaction we receive from this angular cutting of the surface has to do with our delight in crystallized or cubic forms in nature as well as in art. And this pleasure may be connected with our intuitive feeling for the origin of man, in which the formation of cells of geometric shape and their relation to stellar organisms of similar geometric shape is essential. If this interest in the early stages of human development has been called a regression to primitive forms, characteristic of all artistic expression in our time, it should be remembered that it is not the only source for contemporary art; it is inherent in the pantheistic ideas developed during the last centuries in connection with art and culture. Out of the fusion of these two tendencies, which are evidence of a revived sympathy in us for the spiritual forces in nature, the new conceptions of a new epoch are created.

Simplified and crystallized forms, in which we take such delight, are characteristic not only of modern sculpture but of any expression of modern art, architecture as well as painting and drawing. We like drawings with clear-cut forms better than those which have blurred and soft outlines, and in paintings, whether abstract or not, we prefer those which, so to speak, show the crystallization process before our eyes, as those of Feininger and Marin do. Cubistic paintings started out by rendering volumes with clear-cut surfaces, advancing towards a penetration of all volume through constantly changing and shifting planes.

Let us use as first illustration some examples of portrait sculpture with clear-cut planes in mediaeval and modern art (Figs. 44–46). The marble head (Fig. 44) is a detail from the tomb of Cino di Sinibaldi in Pistoia Cathedral, executed by the great Sienese sculptor, Agostino di Giovanni, about 1335. The full-length figure represents the famous university professor lecturing on law. Not only is the construction of the head with its square cheekbones brought out through the broad planes cut into the marble, but we are made better aware of other traits of the head through the underlining straight planes created by the angular strokes of the chisel: the deep-set eyes with a distant look, the fine nose with sensitive nostrils and the slightly open, thin lips uttering words of fundamental importance. If we compare with it the portrait of the poet *Ezra Pound* by Gaudier-Brzeska (Fig. 45), or of *Baudelaire* by Duchamp-Villon (Fig.

46), we shall observe the same stressing of characteristics with the help of planes as in the Gothic head.

Planes are used to the same end as lines in the portrait drawings of great painters like Rembrandt or Daumier, who are able with a few lines to express the distinctive traits of a person. In these lines the borders between planes, which in reality do not exist as lines, are clearly marked and exaggerated. It is true that in nature, too, planes of so simplified a form do not exist, but we come nearer to reality in so far as planes are not separated by lines but by other planes. In both instances, in the drawings on paper and in the portrait sculptures, the artist works with accentuation and exaggeration so as to express the meaning behind the outer aspect, a meaning which we call life.

The primitive wood-carver of masks and ritual figures, especially the African Negro, proceeds in a similar way, using clear-cut planes to give construction to the composition and to express characteristics, but he is less interested in the rendering of individual portrait features, although we know in Negro art of a small number of early portraits of kings.[1] His intention is to assemble in the face only such elements as, in accordance with a primitive, barbarous religion, are apt to subdue the worshiper through the hypnotizing influence of a manifestation of power and of consequent fear. In the mask illustrated (Fig. 47), the vertical line running down from the forehead to the tip of the nose is like a dagger piercing the heart of the devotee with horrible precision; from the narrow slits of the eyes speaks an evil, hidden power; the outlines of the mouth express utter contempt. Planes that give to the face the flatness of a plate and divide nose and mouth into a clear triangle are here combined with such sharp outlines of eyes, eyebrows and forehead as we are accustomed to encounter in works of art on a flat surface as a means of indicating special traits.

Since hypnotic influence emanates mainly from the face, the primitive sculptor creating religious images concentrates upon this part of the human body, entirely so in masks, to a great extent in images, in which the body seems to have been added mainly so as to form a handle for carrying the fetich. The body is always disproportionately small, with accentuation of such parts as could promote the spectator's submission through overpowering sexual influence (Fig. 48). Once in a while we find that the hands are used for emphasizing the impression made by the face, as in a figure from the Belgian Congo (Fig. 49). Then these hands are

1. J. J. Sweeney, *African Negro Art;* 1935.

enlarged to enormous size like the head, while the rest of the body is reduced to rudimentary forms; it is as if the hands want to seize and crush completely the worshiper who stares with horror at the frightening face.

A curious outcome of similar ideas are the stone heads of monumental size rising out of the earth everywhere on small Easter Island (Fig. 50). These sculptures, obviously representing demoniac forces of nature, were greatly admired by modern artists as soon as they were discovered. Undoubtedly Gaudier-Brzeska was influenced by them in his monumental marble head of Ezra Pound, which rests without base directly upon the ground (Fig. 45). But it is significant that, while he gives an individual portrait with characteristic Western features, the stone images from Easter Island were made with the intention of conveying the evil power of demons over man; they are types of terrific strength and ruthless action, with low foreheads, enormous chins and mouths and nostrils full of hate and contempt. From a formal point of view, in their developing angular plastic forms and clear planes, they are superb. It is interesting to compare them with African masks like those reproduced here. In reducing the face to geometric forms with flat planes, we can proceed in two ways: either, by leaving out the hollows of the eyes, reduce the oval of the face to one flat plane upon which the nose is placed like a raised triangle, or, by stressing the hollows of the eyes and the forehead, divide the face into two planes, a higher one marked by the forehead and a lower one consisting of the part of the face below the eyes, a part in which the nose is hardly visible or appears as a very low elevation. The first mask reproduced here (Fig. 47) shows the type in which the nose is prominent and the other portion of the face is one flat plane, the second mask (Fig. 51) illustrates the second type, in which the eyes are prominent. Here the lower part of the face consists of a receding plane, while the upper part, formed by the forehead, is protruding. The Easter Island sculptures (Fig. 50) develop an intermediate state, in which both the eye hollows and the nose are strongly marked, but in such a manner that the plane formed by eyebrows and forehead is on the same level as the tip of the nose, which is broadened in a wide curve corresponding to the curve of the forehead.

These sculptures from the Pacific and from Africa may be compared to some purpose with a portrait of a mediaeval church dignitary, Bishop Wolfhart Roth (died 1302), from his bronze tomb in Augsburg Cathedral (Fig. 52). Here we observe the same use of clear-cut planes for the characterization of a strong representative of a powerful church which at times employed methods of subordination not dissimilar to those practised by priests of primitive tribes. Although the features are less horrible and perhaps less cruel, the expression of contempt and haughtiness is not far removed from that which we see in the religious images of much less civilized countries.

Treating the face of a human figure in one straight plane goes back to late prehistoric times. We find, for instance, idols of marble in the Greek islands at about 2500 B.C. (Fig. 53), which show the faces in the shape of an oval disk in which only the nose is marked by a small elevation in the form of a high triangle. A somewhat similar treatment appears in the faces of the late Chou figurines of clay (Fig. 54), executed at a later epoch. Here also we encounter the first type mentioned above, in which only the nose is indicated, while the eyes are left out altogether.

In connection with the cubistic movement, we find even in the realistic sculpture of Central Europe during the second and third decades of the present century a decided tendency to stress planes in sculpture. In the *Seated Figure* (1915) by Gaudier-Brzeska — a sculptor who is of greater importance as an expression of his time than as an individual — the angular forms of face and body are marked by sharply divided planes (Fig. 55). The expression of the face, as well as the preponderance of the upper part of the body over the lower, reflect the influence of primitive African and primitive American sculptures by which this sculptor was greatly impressed. The *Mermaid* by Kolbe (1922) (Fig. 56) is an excellent example of a nude figure in which every part is treated with a conscious consideration for planes developed out of almost cubic forms. In the *Avenger* by Barlach (Fig. 57), executed at the end of the twenties, the planes are used to give a decided forward movement to a draped figure, a movement also expressed in the face with its simplified angular forms.

Thus we see that the meaning of "planes" in sculpture is necessary for the understanding of the origin of the modern movement, because it signifies not only a constructive, formal element, but also a characteristic related to the spiritual content of the sculptures.

Chapter V

Relief and Sculpture in the Round

Most sculpture in history is relief sculpture

Most of the sculpture of historic periods is relief sculpture. This means not only sculpture in the form of reliefs decorating walls, but also that constructed free from the walls yet related to them. This type of relief sculpture has its own volume but cannot be conceived without an architectural background since it is directed only outwards towards the spectator and at right angles to the wall. Because it protrudes further from the wall than the relief, it provides views from the side as well as from the front.

It would be easy to write a history of relief sculpture from a formal point of view, as its problems are comparatively simple. It would comprise most periods in history and most art-producing nations. There were only two historical epochs in European art — the period of Hellenistic and Roman art and that lasting from the Renaissance to about 1900 — when there was created a type of sculpture which could be seen from all sides. It may seem not worth while to consider these comparatively short periods, during which confusion was introduced into aesthetic conceptions accepted for centuries by entire continents, such as Asia, Africa and America in early periods. Yet we must study these attempts at sculpture in the round, not only because of the chronological nearness to us of the second period in European art, but also because the attempts had some influence upon present-day art.

All early Indian, Chinese and Japanese sculpture is relief sculpture, in the sense of the term used here; so also is Near Eastern sculpture like that of the Sumerians, Assyrians, Babylonians and Persians; all Egyptian and primitive African sculpture, all pre-Columbian American sculpture and, as far as Europe is concerned, all the sculpture of the early Greeks and Etruscans and of the people of the Middle Ages. The formal problems of this type of sculpture may be easily grasped, for they are identical with those of the construction of a wall, since the relief and also relief sculpture detached from the wall form, so to speak, part of it. The relief, as well as detached relief sculpture, is enframed by the wall and has clear planes at its back and front, which are parallel to the wall.

Relief planes essential to relief sculpture

Why do we nowadays dislike reliefs which have no frontal planes? Because they destroy the effect of a solid wall; they break up the continuity of surface and display restlessness and confusion where we expect quietness and harmony. There are, of course, innumerable possibilities for the style and the composition of the relief itself; it can be conceived in different depths (incised, low or high relief) (Figs. 58–61); its plastic forms can be spread over the background in a sporadic manner or can fill the background almost completely; its surface can be treated in a compact, plastic style or in an open, pictorial style; the pattern may run lace-like over the surface, with dark shadows or openings or with mosaic or translucent glass in between. But it is essential always that the relief be shut in on all sides — at back and front, above, below and on the sides — in a caselike framework of geometric planes that are either real or felt to be so by the spectator.

It was only during the nineteenth century that front relief planes in relief sculpture were completely disregarded, thus often causing the architecture behind them to be drowned out by a confusing mass of realistically conceived figures projecting in all directions (Fig. 62). But even in utter decadence certain new ideas are frequently hidden. The tendency to free the relief from the architecture, which we feel underneath the pictorial relief of the impressionistic period, resulted in a new type of relief, which came into existence as a reaction against the previous decline.

New relations between wall and relief sculpture

Since about 1910 it has been possible to find, at first in temporary buildings for world fairs and other exhibitions, single figures or other motifs set as reliefs, sporadically and without frames, into large, empty walls. Here the sculptor returned to the idea of relief planes, but the relief seemed to be independent of the wall, as if it were swimming in space (Fig. 63). The modern idea of creating objects suspended in space in this way penetrated into the art of relief in many modern buildings and produced excellently stylized works of great simplicity and expressiveness, in which we should hardly suspect any connection with the overcrowded realistic compositions of former generations. Yet this type of relief would not have been possible had not the framework of the earlier type, and its connection with the wall, been first destroyed by the impressionistic period.

It was not an accident that, at the same time as this new conception of relief developed, the pre-Romanesque sculptures of the Middle Ages, especially those of the tenth and eleventh centuries, were recognized in their full value. These now seem to us more alive and spontaneous than those of the developed Romanesque style of the twelfth and thirteenth centuries, with precisely stylized forms and more clearly defined framework.[1] We may refer the reader to the great reliefs on the bronze doors of Augsburg Cathedral, executed about 1025, where Biblical or symbolic scenes are represented by individual figures standing free in space with-

1. Harold Picton, *Early German Art and Its Origin;* 1939 (see Chapter V).

out background and conducting themselves in their airy surroundings with a sureness as if they were on solid ground (Fig. 64). An example of this style, of a slightly later epoch, is the bronze relief from the tomb of King Rudolf of Swabia (1080) (Fig. 65) which is already nearer to fully developed Romanesque art in its harder conventionalization and in the addition of the inscription border; yet here too we see the figure standing in empty space without any connection with the framework. The relation to contemporary reliefs arising from similar tendencies may easily be recognized.

It was only a step further for Jacques Lipchitz, in the *Prometheus* group for the auditorium wall of the Ministry of Education of Brazil, to remove the relief altogether from the wall and to suspend it freely in front, so that it throws shadows on the wall behind (Fig. 66). It is a most ingenious solution, suited to the ideas of our time; yet we may ask whether it is a definite solution to the problem of relief or merely a sculpture in the round of the Lipchitz type, which seems actually superimposed upon the wall and appears to defy any connection with it.

Narrative contents of relief: Its variations on themes expressed in the buildings it adorns

If we now consider the content of a relief, we may say that it always accompanies a greater theme expressed in the building to which it belongs. As little in meaning as in form can it exist by itself. The greater theme of the building to which the relief is attached is either expressive of religious or of worldly power, or of both. The subjects of the relief are always narrative — they explain to us, in factual or allegorical stories, the character and cause of this power. In early Oriental art, the reliefs with battle or hunting scenes and processions tell us of the worldly power of the kings ruling in the palaces whose walls or staircases were so decorated. In Egyptian art, the reliefs in the tombs give us a vivid account of the life of the deceased. In Greek, Buddhist and Christian art, the reliefs show scenes from the life of the god or prophet to whom the temple or church was dedicated.

As in music variations are related to the theme, so in reliefs narration is related to the statue of a god or hero who either is near or has to be imagined as spiritually present. In Greek, Roman or early Christian sarcophagi, the deceased to whom the reliefs on the sides are dedicated are often represented alive in the attitude of praying or of sitting upon the throne, like those of the Anjou kings in Naples (Fig. 59), and the reliefs decorating the sarcophagi show allegorical figures or scenes from the life of the deceased. This idea lived on until the nineteenth century in statues, monuments or tombs of rulers or war heroes, which are decorated with reliefs that tell their story.

In contemporary art, relief preserves its function as narrative accompaniment to a larger theme when it decorates the official or private buildings of industry. Examples in this country are, for instance, Carl Milles' entertaining reliefs on the Radio Station building of the Detroit News, and those in Rockefeller Center, while in several of Milles' earlier works the narrative reliefs decorate monuments to legendary or historical personalities, in the manner of mediaeval art.

Origin of detached relief sculpture

A connection similar to that between relief and architecture exists between detached relief sculpture and its architectural background. Although the architectural frame is in this case always imaginary, the sculpture consists of clearly divided geometric forms which are taken over from the architecture behind it. Its origin may be compared to that of stars that were at one time connected to another star and that upon separation kept the same form and rhythm.

If we take as examples detached relief sculpture from Egyptian or archaic Greek art, we can imagine the standing statues to have been born out of columns or pillars, the seated ones out of the combination of vertically and horizontally directed profiles of the buildings of which they are part, such as mouldings, bases of columns and especially stairs leading up to temples (Figs. 67, 68). The stone seats or thrones upon which these figures sit seem to initiate a connection with the temple stairways by their providing a sudden change from vertical to horizontal direction. The human figures placed upon the steps follow in their angular poses the same course.

It would be easy to give other instances from Asiatic or pre-Columbian American art, but we shall mention only the statues of gods from the hieroglyphic stairway at Copan, a great work of mediaeval Mayan art (Fig. 68a). These figures actually sat upon the steps of the high stairway leading up to the sacrificial altar; their position and style is perfectly adapted to the architectural background.

In accordance with these geometric architectural forms, there exists in free-standing relief sculpture not only the possibility of alternating from the vertical to the horizontal, but also from the front to side view, the latter constituting a sudden change taking place at right angles. The statues should be observed either precisely from the front — this, in the first place, was the view intended by the sculptor — or in complete profile (Figs. 69, 70).

Lack of plastic values in photographs

Unfortunately, if we study these sculptures from photographs, we are often misled by the wrong point of view adopted by the photographer, which presents the statues from between angles, although in this instance

60. *B. Antelami, 12th century*

61. *T'ang Dynasty, 10th century*

62. *W. M. Hunt*   63. *E. Scharff*

64. *Augsburg, 11th century*

65. *Merseburg, 11th century*

66. *J. Lipchitz*

The author and publisher inadvertently neglected to ask Mr. Jacques Lipchitz
for permission to reproduce this illustration before going to press; the artist
later refused to give his consent, and we have regretfully withdrawn the
plate. The reader can find this same illustration on page 8 of Volume XII, No. 2,
of the Museum of Modern Art Bulletin for November, 1944.

67, } *Queen Hat-shepsut,*
68. } *c. 1485* B.C.

68 a. *Mayan, Copan*

69, 70. *Ikhnaton, c. 1380* B.C.

71, 72. *Egyptian, 7th–6th century*

73. *Assyrian, 9th century*

74 a–c. *A. Vittoria*

75 a, b. *Porcelain Group*

76. *C. Milles*

77. H'an Period

78. *H. K. Brown*

79. *A. Saint-Gaudens*

80. *Roman, 1st century* B.C.

81. *Bamberg, 13th century*

82 a. *Verona, 14th century*

82 b. *Verona, 14th century*

83. *Milan, 14th century*

the photographer alone is not to blame. Indeed, sculptures of the relief type look better in photographs if seen with strong contrasts of light and shadow, from between the angles instead of exactly from the front (Figs. 68, 70). If taken from the front, in the photograph (Figs. 67, 69) the plastic values of the foreshortenings are lost which we feel to be very essential in the original. Because we have two eyes and see the forms in a narrow angle from two sides as in a stereopticon, we can appreciate these foreshortenings, which are of great importance to the sculptor in his endeavor to create depth and space. The apparatus of the photographer, however, sees the object, so to speak, only with one eye, that is, in the flat. Sculptures cannot therefore be judged correctly from photographs, in regard to their realization of volume.

As detached relief sculpture is related to the wall in the same manner as actual relief, it follows the same principles in regard to relief planes as the relief itself does. In this case, however, side relief planes will be added to the front relief planes, because, as we have said before, free-standing relief sculpture can also be seen in profile. A statue of this type created in the archaic or mediaeval periods is inconceivable without planes on front and sides (Figs. 69, 70).

Front view of human figure well adapted to relief sculpture

One reason why relief sculpture (in the wide sense in which we use it) is so important in the history of mankind is probably because the human figure, which has been the main motif in historical periods, by nature lends itself well to relief representation. We are more accustomed to looking at people from the front than from the side and sometimes are not even aware of the character of the profile of a close friend. Our customs increase this habit; to look straight into the face of the person we meet is considered a sign of honesty; to study the profile of a person who sits at our side in a public conveyance is considered impolite and even suspicious; a back view of others is of no interest to most people. We have, therefore, been accustomed, from ancient times, to consider the sculpture of a human being from the front. If man walked on all fours, as he no doubt originally did, his profile would be more conspicuous than the front view, as we see in sculptured representations of animals with four legs. Such animals as horses, bulls, lions, cats and so on, are frequently used in reliefs by early sculptors, but rarely in free-standing sculptures, in which the front views had to be emphasized, because they were directed towards the worshipers advancing to the buildings in front of which these sculptures were placed or imagined.

It is characteristic that the Egyptian sculptor in fashioning a cat (Fig. 71) had it rest on its hind legs, so as to obtain a better front view than would have been possible if he had represented it walking. The side view, more compact, produces thus the greater volume necessary for a free-standing sculpture. For the same reason the early Greek sculptor represented the sphinx in an upright sitting position. The Egyptians, even when they showed the sphinx resting on all four legs, managed to make the front view more important than the side by increasing the size of the head, surrounding it by a flat head-dress and collar, stressing the verticals of the plane through the middle of the chest and by shortening the heavy front claws, as we see in the granite sphinx representing Amenemhet III. If for religious reasons it was imperative to represent a four-legged animal in a standing position, as in the case of the god Hathor as a bull (Fig. 72), the Egyptians filled the open space between the legs with straight walls and placed a human figure with clear frontal planes beneath the head, thus stressing the front view of the sculpture. Here is an example which demonstrates conspicuously the natural adaptability of the human figure to the frontal relief sculpture of which the early sculptor was so fond. When he had to represent man standing or sitting, he could easily produce a closed wall, in the sense of a relief plane; not so with a standing animal on four legs, whose front legs are by nature set somewhat apart. This last point will be studied in connection with the equestrian statue; we mention here only the strange winged lion from the palace of Asurnasirpal, in the Metropolitan Museum of Art, in which the Assyrian sculptor (ninth century B.C.) represented the animal from front and side, yet stressed the front view by transforming the head into a human face with long beard and by placing the front legs close together. While the lion is depicted in profile in a walking position, thus adding life to this view, if seen from the front it stands motionless in an impressive, majestic posture. This double view could be achieved only by giving the animal five instead of four legs (Fig. 73).

The comparative simplicity in the construction of detached relief sculpture, as we find it in so many epochs and countries — a simplicity which amounts to an avoidance of all difficult formal problems, particularly in Far Eastern sculpture — is demanded by the importance of spiritual content in this type of sculpture. As a rule, it may be said that the more intensely a sculptor is occupied with the spiritual side of his work the more he is satisfied with an uncomplicated formal composition. When the Chinese sculptor made a Buddha statue, either a standing or a seated one, and intended it to be placed against a wall, he would use the same formula over and over again. He was not interested in a substantial change of this formula, but tried to express his own conception in the differing spiritual attitudes of the figure, which could be accomplished by slight variations in facial expression or position of body, legs and arms, without altering the general outline of the sculpture or its relief planes.

A similar procedure may be observed among the early sculptors of Christian images. It was impossible — on account of the nature of the subject — to change essentially the Crucifixion as to its plastic formula, yet there are hundreds of variations in the spiritual expression caused by slight changes in the position of Christ or of his facial characteristics. The Madonna statuette, too, either standing or enthroned, was early developed into a standard type, from which the sculptor might start in developing his own ideas without being able to wander too far astray from the original religious themes whose proper rendering was his first aim.

The harmony in early art between architecture and relief sculpture is due in some degree to the fact that architect and sculptor were usually one and the same person. As soon as we have documentary evidence of individual personalities in mediaeval architecture, we learn that the sculptors whose names are outstanding were also architects. In Italy, for instance, in the fourteenth century, Niccolo and Giovanni Pisano in Pisa, Arnolfo di Cambio in Florence, Lorenzo Maitani in Siena, masters who built some of the greatest Gothic churches in Italy, at the same time decorated them with their own sculptures. But since the Renaissance, the two professions have separated more and more, until in the nineteenth century sculpture without architectural background became the rule.

Sculpture in the round during the Renaissance

With Donatello began the tendency of freeing the relief from the architectural background, although he himself was still one of the greatest relief sculptors of all times and never thought of even a free-standing figure without a real or an imaginary background.

Michelangelo was the first to conceive statues free from the wall in an all-round aspect. In his early years he made two reliefs which still had clear, front relief planes, but it is characteristic of him that he later abandoned this type altogether, to work in the round. All his figures develop away from the relief conception, which meant a gradual giving up of the idea of clear-cut relief planes. The corners, where in relief sculpture the two planes — the side and the front — meet at sharp angles, are smoothed down and curved so much that the eye without interruption is led from one side to the other. The turning point of the two views now becomes an essential part of the sculpture. Through its curves the spectator is forced to follow the movement around the corners and is not satisfied until he has seen the statue from all sides.

The spiral movement characteristic of the followers of Michelangelo, like Giovanni da Bologna and Alessandro Vittoria (Fig. 74: a–c), led in the art of the Baroque and Rococo periods to a breaking up of the forms and a dissolving of the silhouette. It is as if the quickly turning movements of the figures caused the discarding of certain parts of the volume. From the moment when sculpture in the round is fully developed, we may no longer speak of relief planes. Even so, there will always exist some kind of imaginary geometric encasement which encloses the work, an encasement no longer in the shape of straight planes, but of hollows or vaults ending in curved outlines.

However, this imaginary encasement is of less importance than the framework in the case of relief sculpture. Since the sculptor has to create a strong movement within his composition in order to bring the spectator under the spell of its circular motion, the whole character of the sculpture undergoes a change. While formerly its composition was static, it becomes dynamic, and this inner, essential force, which radiates in different directions, is now the focus of all the attention, while the framework acquires secondary importance.

The spiral, screwlike or radial movement, which was necessitated by realistic sculpture in the round, resulted in a very complicated sort of composition. Combined with emotional content, it could be mastered only by geniuses such as Michelangelo, Bernini or Rodin. Otherwise it became a matter of virtuosity, which merely produced works of decorative quality without any deeper meaning, as we see in many of the often charming and playful compositions of the Rococo. Whether these were executed in life-size figures of marble or bronze for fountains or gardens, as in Rome or Versailles, or as small porcelain groups by German factories like Meissen, Nymphenburg, Höchst and Frankenthal, the greatest effort was always concentrated upon a display of clever, formal arrangement, opening the volume in radial directions in an all-round conception, while the subjects revived classical, allegorical or mythological themes with little meaning for us or even for contemporaries.

That an all-round composition soon developed from Michelangelo's representation of one individual figure into groups of several figures, or even into an arrangement with masses of figures, possessed a practical reason from a formal point of view. To express circular movement in one figure demanded the spiritual tenseness and skill of a Michelangelo if it were not to become mannerism, as it did in many of his followers. It was much easier to divide this movement among different figures, which were connected by a rhythm swinging at intervals from the inside of the composition to the outside. The individual figure, then, did not need to be exaggeratedly twisted around itself, but took up only a part of the circular movement, which was continued by the figure next to it. To illustrate the point, we reproduce a Meissen porcelain group of the middle of the eighteenth century (Fig. 75: a, b) which, when displayed upon a dining-table, is to be seen from all sides. The turning movement of the two cupids and the lion upon which they rest leads us from one figure to the other, at the same time unfolding another side of the group towards the spectator wherever he may be sitting.

The circular arrangement in fountain groups of the seventeenth and eighteenth centuries, with their all-round aspect, is too well known to require description. It was at a time of growing interest in pantheism that the sculpturing of fountains and garden figures reached its greatest height. Although the content of the compositions may have lacked spiritual quality, the fact that they were created for an out-of-door enjoyment related to an artificial garden architecture bears witness to a subconscious connection with the pantheistic tendencies of the time.

A continuation of this out-of-door sculpture in the round is seen in the work of Carl Milles (Fig. 76). The subject-matter of his fountains is taken, like those of earlier periods, from classical mythology, and their all-round conception is similar too, although the feeling for volume has increased again in accordance with the inclinations of his generation. It was this generation, the one to which Maillol and Kolbe also belonged, that revolted against the impressionism of Rodin.

But the important fact is that the content of these figures is imbued with a conscious striving for a closer, spiritual connection with nature. In Milles' Orpheus fountain, the surrounding figures not only listen to the music, which is symbolic of the sounds of nature, but seem to be so carried away by it that their souls become one with nature. Whether this is expressed under cover of a return to classical simplicity, as also in Maillol's art, is unimportant—a complete freeing of forms cannot be expected in any transitional period;[2] but it is essential that the content of these sculptures is expressive of the same cosmic ideas towards which the most modern sculptors of our day are striving.

2. I should like to mention in this connection that Richard Strauss, who belonged to the same generation as Milles, told me once that he regarded himself as an artist of a transitional period, comparing himself to Tintoretto, who connected the Renaissance with the Baroque in painting. He remarked that Wagner's *Tristan* was the end of a development, after which a new goal had to be set. The reaching of this goal, he said, will only be possible after passing through a transitional period in which the old and new forms have not yet been clearly separated.

Chapter VI

Horse and Rider

Equestrian statues in East and in West

After these generalizations it may be well to demonstrate by concrete example the development from relief sculpture to sculpture in the round. The history of the equestrian statue will serve for this purpose. It is a purely Western affair, for in the East, individualism never developed to the same degree as in the West, so that to have erected individual monuments to war heroes or statesmen would have been impossible; nor could Eastern religious figures have been represented on horseback as was St. George, in whom was embodied the whole idea of adventure and personal courage paramount in the European Middle Ages. There exist, however, a sufficient number of small equestrian figures found in early Chinese tombs to give an idea of the Eastern conception of horse and rider; and the manner in which a monument to an individual hero could be erected in the East may be shown by the tumulus tomb of the second century B.C. — here reproduced (Fig. 77) — dedicated to Houo K'iu-ping. It represents the warrior's favorite horse, without the rider, standing upon a fallen enemy, the group being conceived as a blocklike relief of broad, monumental forms seen against the background of the tumulus and a wide landscape.

The execution of equestrian statues presents many problems from the sculptor's point of view. The horse with its elongated body looks best from the side, although the wide opening between front and hind legs is an obstacle not easy to overcome. The open spaces, of course, offer no difficulties in the case of relief sculpture, where the background of the relief or the wall of a building closes the openings. Mainly for this reason the horse has been used from early times in relief representations; not until relatively late in history do we encounter free-standing equestrian statues.

The horse's body rests on four thin legs, which, like those of the deer, are made for running. When the horse stands still or walks, the weight of the body seems heavy in comparison to the supports. As an equestrian statue is usually placed at the top of a high pedestal, the uninteresting under side of the horse is the most prominent, and the irregularly shaped open spaces between the legs counteract the sense of volume expressed in the animal's torso.

Equestrian statues in the nineteenth century

If we pass around a monument — referring here to those of the last century — the legs of the horse, which are silhouetted against the sky, appear even thinner than they actually are and cross one another in a confusing manner, so that the little plastic value they have is reduced to nothing. We expect from the shape of the pedestal, and the inscription usually decorating the front, that the front view will be the best. It is generally the worst; for not only do the legs not form a compact volume when seen from there, but neither do the head and neck of the horse; besides they interfere with the head of the rider behind them. Nowhere do we find planes or curves restful to the eye; if the movement is accentuated, it is not strong enough to force us to overlook the weakness of the construction. Usually the side views are better, although an attempt is hardly ever made to solve the problem of the empty spaces between the legs. Some Baroque and contemporary sculptors have treated such open spaces either by relating them to other open spaces in the composition or by transforming them into shadow hollows which create the illusion of volume. Sometimes it happens that the view from behind the monument a little to one side is the best — but who wants to look at a monument always from the back?

These impressions can be easily verified by any of the numerous nineteenth-century equestrian statues in squares in New York, Philadelphia, Washington or Boston. The American sculptor alone was not entirely responsible for these results; he was the product of a period in which all artists had less feeling for volume than at any other time. In Europe, too, at this same time there were produced as many, if not more, bad equestrian statues. The courage with which the American sculptors undertook this most difficult problem was out of proportion to their experience, which was of very short duration compared to the long development of the equestrian statue in Europe. If a genius like Leonardo, in spite of many brilliant sketches and models, never came to a definite solution, we cannot expect to find perfect results in a young country, especially when sculpture was the last of the arts to come to life.

Brown's Washington

Let us study two of the most famous American equestrian statues: that of Washington by Henry Kirke Brown (Fig. 78) in Union Square, New York (finished with the help of young John Quincy Adams Ward in 1856) and that of General Sherman by Saint-Gaudens (Fig. 79) on 59th Street and Fifth Avenue, New York, which was unveiled in 1903.

The first is indeed remarkable if we consider that it was the first equestrian statue of Washington cast in this country, preceded by only a few years by the first bronze equestrian statue in America, that of General Jackson by Clark Mills (1853) in Washington. With all its awkwardness the *Washington* impresses us as a work of dignity and heroic character; it shows the sculptor to have been occupied with a sincere effort to give volume and movement to both horse and rider. The best and only successful view of this statue is the one in profile from the east (Fig. 78). The front view is not so successful, although we can at least look straight into the face of Washington, a fact worthy of mention, since in many equestrian statues the horse's head is raised so high that from this view it is impossible to see much of the rider. However, the horse's head and legs here form a disturbing mass of unplastic motifs. If we stand off-center on the western side of the figure — a natural position, since we like to see more of the figure of Washington, who is slightly turned to this side — it looks as if the horse had only three legs, and a large empty space appears under his belly on the further side; the torso of the horse seems hanging unbalanced in the air.

The model was obviously the Marcus Aurelius equestrian statue from the Capitol in Rome, probably known to Brown from his short stay in Italy and from engravings. But the original statue has on each side the near background of two Renaissance palaces and also was placed (by Michelangelo) upon a much lower pedestal, so that we feel as if we were standing almost on an even height with the horse. Thus we do not see it so much from below, especially as the legs are shorter and heavier. The horse is in rather fast motion, which distracts the spectator's eyes from the open spaces between the legs. But although more successful in some ways, this late Roman work does not give so perfect a solution of the problem that it deserves to have been copied as frequently as has been done. It is known to have been saved from Christian wrath and destruction only because it was believed in the Middle Ages to represent Constantine the Great. Probably (in the classical periods) there existed many other equestrian statues, which were conceived on sounder principles.

Saint-Gaudens'
Sherman

Saint-Gaudens' monument of Sherman belongs to the impressionistic period and has therefore less feeling for volume than Brown's statue. Like most of Saint-Gaudens' sculptures, it looks as if it were made of cardboard which could be blown over by a strong wind. It is full of rather exquisite decorative details, but lacks the large planes for the eye to rest upon that we might expect from a work so clearly conceived as relief sculpture. An allegorical figure leading the rider to victory is introduced so as to cover, partly at least, the open spaces around the lower section of the horse, but in the side view this figure's enormous wings cover some of the most solid portions of the horse's body. From the front the victory angel looks well, but not so the rider, whose head is completely obscured by the horse's head, even if viewed from a considerable distance. The artist was obviously of the opinion that fast movement might compensate for lack of volume; it should at any rate be remarked that the monument is consistent in all parts in this respect. But unfortunately the often-praised temperament which Saint-Gaudens is supposed to have inherited from his partly French ancestry does not alone make an artist. In our time, at least, it is difficult to admire an art which lacks that quality so essential to sculpture, the feeling for volume, replacing it by a Whistlerian taste for spirited outline and decorative elegance. That it was possible even in the impressionistic period to combine pictorial treatment and strong movement with a fundamental sense of volume has been proved by Rodin.

The opinion advanced in histories of American sculpture that sculpture in this country came into its own only after the World's Fair of 1876, which resulted in a constant drifting of American students to Paris, is very questionable. French influence was disastrous to many American sculptors, whose temperament was entirely different from that of the French. Those who resisted this movement, some of the best working long before the time of the World's Fair of 1876, showed more character and created, in spite of some awkwardness, more interesting work than those who managed only to produce superficial and completely empty imitations of French sculptures.

The best American equestrian statues are those by John Quincy Adams Ward, who kept the solidity of his forms even in a period when most principles of good sculpture were thrown to the winds. It was characteristic of him that for his last statue, that of General Hancock, he found the model for the horse after long search in front of a beer wagon, a heavy Belgian farm horse, which he managed to have moved to his studio. In this statue he presents the horse standing still, with front and hind legs close together, so that a compact effect is achieved, almost as in some mediaeval statues. If, in spite of these good qualities, Ward's equestrian statues are not as satisfactory from a formal point of view as those he did of individual figures such as the soldier from the 7th Regiment, Horace Greeley or Henry Ward Beecher, the reason is the impossible problem posed by the idea of the equestrian monument as conceived in the nineteenth century. When Montgomery Schuyler, speaking about John Quincy Adams Ward's equestrian statues, says, "The equestrian statue is doubtless the most grateful of problems in portraiture for the right sculptor,"[1] he is far from the point. As an all-round statue, it is the most ungrateful task imaginable; it can be overcome only with rather artificial means by a highly sophisticated art, which fortunately Ward's was not.

1. *Putnam's Magazine*, VI, Sept. 1909, pp. 643–656.

The mediaeval sculptors of equestrian statues were the most successful, because they treated the figure as relief sculpture in close connection with architecture in an almost abstract manner, subordinating the composition to a geometric pattern which included the open spaces, relating them to the solid masses of the statue. If we except the Marcus Aurelius statue, it seems likely that the classical solution in Greek and Roman art anticipated this conception.

Equestrian statues in classical art

There are three Roman equestrian statues of the early Imperial period preserved in the Naples Museum: one in bronze, of which the horse is, however, almost completely restored, two in marble (Fig. 80). They go back obviously to the same Greek type of the fifth or fourth century, which must have been a detached relief group placed in a court surrounded by architecture. An imaginary rectangle can be drawn around the statues as if they were reliefs set in a wall, and each section of the group can be divided into squares or triangles. The position of the outstretched arm is probably nearer to the original in the two marble versions. In these the right arm is slightly raised, corresponding in a contraposto movement to the forward-stepping left foot of the horse, the angle of which is exactly the same as that of the raised arm. The reins led originally from the horse's mouth horizontally to the rider's left hand, thus dividing the horse's neck into different geometric sections, of which the base is continued along the back of the horse.

in mediaeval art

We do not hear of any equestrian statue in France during the Middle Ages, but two of great beauty are — or were until recently — still in existence in Germany: the famous Bamberg rider (Fig. 81) and the statue on the market square in Magdeburg, both of the thirteenth century. It is characteristic of the mediaeval conception that these horsemen are obviously not portraits but figures of symbolic character, and for this reason they are similar in their idealized type, although the Bamberg rider possibly represents a saint (St. Stephen of Hungary), that of Magdeburg, the worldly power of the emperor revealed in the act of delivering certain privileges to the city government. Mediaeval also is their close connection with church architecture and the reduction of their parts to simple geometric forms; the Bamberg statue is placed upon a large console on the wall inside the cathedral, the Magdeburg rider stands upon a lofty pedestal, originally of Gothic structure, under a baldaquin carried by pillars. We therefore cannot see the Magdeburg statue as a whole but as if it were inside a cage, broken up by the verticals of the pillars which at the same time divide in sections the empty space around the horses' bodies. Both the Bamberg and Magdeburg statues are conceived in compact masses of geometric outlines, the surfaces treated in large planes, while the faces of the riders express that spiritual nobility typical of the best sculptures of the Middle Ages.

The equestrian statues we encounter in the fourteenth century in Lombardy are similar in composition, although executed in marble, not in sandstone as were the German ones. Three of them adorn the Scaliger tombs in Verona, one of which is placed inside an architectural framework similar to that of the Magdeburg rider; a fourth represents the Duke of Milan, Bernabo Visconti (Fig. 83). These statues are somewhat less dependent upon the Gothic architecture next to them, although they are still of the type we call detached relief sculpture. Differing in subject-matter from the German riders, they are erected above the tombs of individuals and begin to have portrait-like features. We know that in Italy the realistic portrait developed in the fourteenth and fifteenth centuries, at a time when many small principalities were ruled by despots who assembled at their courts persons representative of trade and culture in all phases.

Leaving aside the best-known of the Veronese equestrian monuments, that of Can Grande, as its place in history is not certain, owing to many restorations and changes in position, we reproduce the two most characteristic of the end of the fourteenth century: Can Signorio of Verona (died 1374) (Fig. 82a, b) and Bernabo Visconti of Milan (died 1385) (Fig. 83), which to my mind are both by the same hand, Bonino da Campione (the first is signed by him, the second goes well stylistically with his later Milanese works). The Can Signorio statue is placed at the top of a high Gothic structure decorated with many allegorical figures, a structure which contains, in the lower section, the sarcophagus. The Visconti statue comes nearer to the modern idea of an equestrian monument, as the statue forms the essential part of the construction, and the sarcophagus, supported by short and heavy pillars, is reduced to the size of a base. It was executed during the lifetime of the tyrannical Duke of Milan and, on his orders, placed behind the main altar of St. Giovanni in Conca, so that the worshipers kneeling in front of it could not avoid seeing the dread figure behind the altar.

The massive forms of these two equestrian statues still possess the stabile character of mediaeval sculpture, although the portrait-like features point to the beginning of the Renaissance. Both horses are for practical and aesthetic reasons supported underneath in the center by a short pillar, which in the Visconti monument is concealed by two female allegorical figures originally also attached to the earlier Magdeburg rider.

The realistic style in Italian art during the second half of the fifteenth century is represented by the famous equestrian statues in bronze by Donatello and Verrocchio, the *Gattamelata* and the *Colleoni*. The more imitative of nature the portraits of horse and rider become, the more lively is the movement, the more detached is the conception from a connection with architecture. It should not be forgotten, however, that both these statues are still composed essentially for side view and cannot be imagined without the immediate proximity of the Gothic churches against whose walls their effect can be measured.

The tendency towards an all-round sculpture begins to take shape in the *Colleoni,* with its contraposto movement in the daring position of horse and rider. About twenty years later, Verrocchio's great pupil Leonardo created—on paper at least (Fig. 84)—in the second commission he received for an equestrian statue, one which should have been seen from all sides without architectural background. Only sketches for the Trivulzio monument, and a bronze model of the horse, have been preserved, but they give sufficient idea of the composition, with its complex turning of the bodies of horse and rider towards different sides. Leonardo's inventive mind and high intellect were necessary in order to find the solution for this difficult problem, the execution of which could be imagined only in a sculpture of his pictorial style. In the Trivulzio group, motion is intensified by representing the horse in a rearing attitude; the movement of horse and rider — their heads turned in opposite directions — expresses great dynamic force. A crouching figure of a defeated enemy is added beneath the feet of the horse, with a double task of filling in the hole created by the raised front legs and of offering to the spectator a new and unexpected view, this figure too being turned around in a direction opposite to that of the rider. In this monument the artist adapted the composition to the addition of a sarcophagus, which was to be placed inside the base; and it should be observed what good use Leonardo made of the presence of the sarcophagus by opening the base on all sides above, thus relating the open space created here to the open spaces around the horse's lower part. No sculptor of equestrian statues in later periods took up this idea, perhaps for fear of decreasing too much the solidity of the base.

How closely the problem of the equestrian statue was at this time related to the mediaeval one of St. George killing the dragon is shown in a small bronze model in *cire perdue,* probably taken from a wax sketch by Leonardo (Fig. 85). This shows a group in an all-round aspect, in the style of the High Renaissance, in which the dragon in front of the rearing horse takes the place of the prostrate figure in the equestrian statue of Trivulzio.

The contemporaneity of ideas is proved by a comparison with the fantastic and fascinating life-size wooden group of St. George and the Dragon, contemporary with Leonardo's sketches, made in the northern part of Europe by Bernt Notke, of Lübeck, for a church in Stockholm (Fig. 86a). The Chinese-looking dragon of enormous size is fiercely twisted around itself, turning its dangerous fangs like a porcupine in all directions, while the beautifully decorated horse moves its head fearfully away, leaving the knight a clear view for striking the dragon's head with the sword. The brilliantly painted trappings of the horse, the armor of the saint and the combination of wood and deer-horn used for the dragon give this fairy-like apparition of Germanic fantasy an almost surrealist effect. The front view (Fig. 86b) creating strange Baroque outlines, yet producing at the same time a rich plastic effect of compact masses, should be compared with the unsuccessful front views of most nineteenth-century equestrian statues.

in the Baroque period

The equestrian statues of the Baroque age from the late sixteenth to the late eighteenth century followed alternately the idea of the fast-walking horse, as in Leonardo's first sketch of an equestrian statue (the Sforza monument), or the idea of the rearing horse, similar to his models for the Trivulzio monument. Pietro Tacca, for instance, a pupil of Giovanni da Bologna, tried the former position for his statue of Philip IV in Madrid (1635–1640) (Fig. 87), then decided on the rearing horse, in accordance with the king's wishes (Fig. 88). The model with the walking horse, in the Detroit Museum (Fig. 87), shows the body of the horse pushed together from the two ends so as to give it more volume, imitating yet exaggerating by these means an idea of Verrocchio's. As in other Baroque equestrian statues, the horse's mane and tail fall down in long and massive waves; the tail thus closes the opening between the hind legs and helps to form a clear plane for a direct front and back view. How much these Baroque masters still worked with relief planes is evident from the back view of Tacca's statue (Fig. 89), as well as in Girardon's Louis XIV (Fig. 90), of which a reduced original replica is also in the Detroit Museum (the large original standing in the Place Vendôme was destroyed during the French Revolution). In both statues we may observe that the back view is developed in two vertical planes, which are separated by the horizontal of the horse's back, the further plane being formed by the straight wall of the rider's back, the nearer one by the horse's hind legs and tail.

It is not to the point to follow through in detail the various equestrian

84. *Leonardo da Vinci*

85. *Florentine, 16th century*

86 a and 86 b. *Bernt Notke, 1488*

87.
88. } *P. Tacca*
89.

90. *F. Girardon*

91. *L. Bernini*
92. *E. M. Falconet*

94. *C. Milles*

93. *G. Borglum*

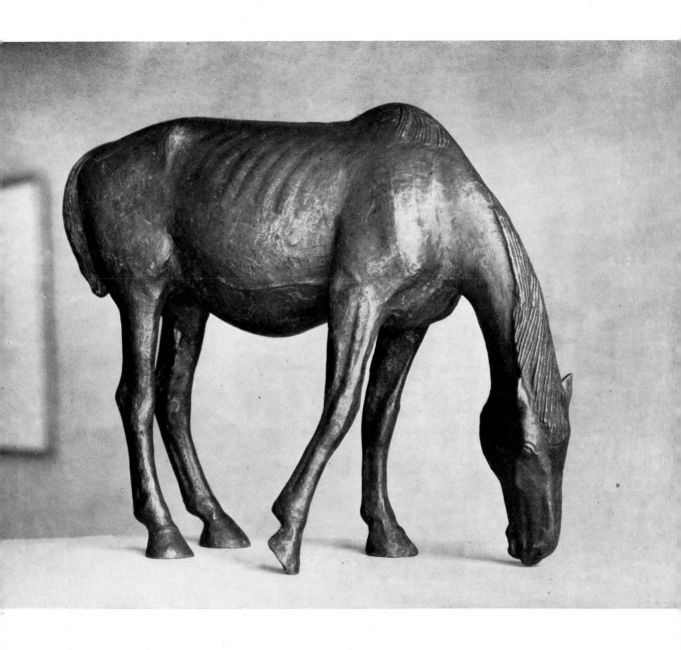

95. *G. Marcks*

96. *H. Gaudier-Brzeska*

97. *R. Duchamp-Villon*

98. *M. Callery*

120

99. *Men-an-Tol, Cornwall*

100. *Menec, Brittany*

101. *Tombs, Ming Dynasty*

102. *Tomb, T'ang Kao-tsong*

103, 104. *Henry Moore*

105, 106, 107. *Henry Moore*

125

108, 109. *Henry Moore*

110. *Aztec*

111, 112. *Chinese, c. 1500* B.C.

113. *J. B. Flannagan*

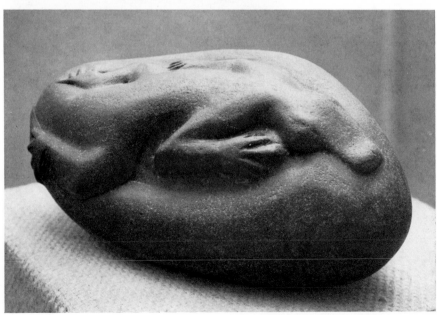

114. *Egyptian, c. 1400* B.C.
115. *Chinese, c. 520* B.C.

statues of the walking-horse type, of which the most important, after Tacca, are the two statues of the Farneses in Piacenza, by Francesco Mocchi (ca. 1648), the above-mentioned statue of Louis XIV by Girardon and the two German ones by Andreas Schlüter (Elector Frederick William, 1698–1703, in Berlin) and by Grupello (Elector Johann Wilhelm, 1703–1711, in Düsseldorf). All were created within fifty years of each other, at the height of the Baroque age, and therefore combine massive volume with strong movement stressed with the help of the flowing masses of the horse's mane and tail and of the rider's costume and hair. The most characteristic example, although perhaps not the best, is that of Alessandro Farnese by Mocchi, in which the composition has the character of a flag on a high pole torn by a storm.

We are more interested in the examples of statues of the rearing-horse type, because they better overcome the difficulty of the heavy torso placed upon slender supports, by connecting the horse's hind part with the ground. Tacca's model (Fig. 87) differs from Leonardo's (Fig. 84) in that the horse is not in the wildly jumping mood of battle but in a carefully trained riding-school position, which exhibited Philip IV's ability as a rider *à l'étiquette*. The effect of a compact mass rising diagonally from the earth is, however, the same, except that the vertical tendency is here stressed by the parallel lines of the horse's front and the rider's straight attitude, thus giving to the king a severe and elevated expression.

It is understandable that Louis XIV did not like the beautiful model for his equestrian statue by Bernini (Fig. 91), although it is certainly worthy of the genius of the greatest Baroque sculptor. It was conceived as a romantic fantasy around a youthful knight of adventurous temperament, but it has nothing of the stiff ceremonial which the Sun King preferred and which Girardon expressed in his less interesting statue, after Bernini's ideas had been discarded. Bernini's statue was executed in marble and transported to France, but here the head was changed into one of Marcus Curtius by Girardon, and the group later disappeared in the park of Versailles as a garden figure.

Bernini explained the rock beneath the horse in his model as symbolizing the culminating point to which the Sun King had ascended without difficulty, but it is obvious that the artist added it for formal reasons, so as to close the unfortunate openings between the horse's legs and to give support for the execution in marble. Thus, together with the torso of the animal, a solid block is formed in the center of the group, around which the open parts of horse and rider unfold in a brilliant radial motion.

The last great equestrian statue of the Baroque age was created by

Falconet in his monument to Peter the Great of Russia, in Leningrad (1766–1778) (Fig. 92). The composition of this statue develops forcefully in a diagonal direction, starting with the horse's tail touching the ground, and increases in a widening angle towards the mass of horse and rider who seem to climb a steep mountain slope at a triumphant gallop. A heavy stone base cut with the same diagonal outlines from a monolith was found, at the sculptor's order, after long search in Finland and was with great difficulty transported to St. Petersburg. Its massive form adds considerably to the effect of the monument. As in the case of Bernini, the sculptor succeeded in creating a compact kernel from which the group rises with the dynamic force characteristic of the Baroque masters of all-round sculpture. (It is interesting to note that the composition of the first American equestrian statue by Clark Mills, representing General Jackson, is based upon that of Falconet's.)[2]

The many monuments of the nineteenth century added nothing new to the equestrian statue. The real popularity of this type of monument was at an end just as it came more than ever into common use. Neither its formal possibilities, which were exhausted, nor its content have value for our time, which strives for greater simplicity and vaster ideals than the commemoration of individual personalities in lifelike portraits of military character. Besides, kings, presidents and generals no longer ride horseback in victory parades, but use for such occasions the more comfortable automobile.

Horse and rider in modern art

This does not mean that the motif of horse and rider will disappear from the repertory of the sculptor. The horse, that shy, timid, yet powerful, animal, has for long periods of history been closely related to man. Its usefulness, its easy tractability and its hidden strength will always make it — either alone or with rider — a tempting subject to the artist who tries to understand the mysteries of nature. And no longer does the rider need to be a tyrant of historical importance, skilfully overpowering and taming his mount, but may be simply an appreciative friend.

As an example of new directions in a transitional period, which at the same time take off from a last development in the creation of horse-and-rider groups, we may mention a small bronze group by Gutzon Borglum (Fig. 93), a very gifted sculptor but with a tendency towards empty virtuosity, and also the life-size group of *Folke Filbyter* by Carl Milles (Fig. 94), which stands on a much higher aesthetic level.

2. This was observed by Lorado Taft. But it is not so well known that Thomas Ball's equestrian statue of Washington in Boston (1860–64) is clearly based upon Rauch's Frederick the Great in Berlin (1841–51).

These groups show that in the first decades of the twentieth century the sense of volume and the desire for a closed compositional form was growing again. Borglum succeeds in composing the two figures of horse and cowboy in the form of a ball, with a swirling movement of both, so that the group can be seen from all sides. Milles finds a quieter and more monumental solution but also bases his group on a narrow stem by placing the horse's legs close together in a small space, while opening the composition above through a decided turn of the head of both horse and rider in different directions. The sudden halt of the horse and the leaning-forward movement of the rider are motivated by the charming northern legend here illustrated, in which the old king is searching for his son in a wild forest. This original, although complicated, solution of an old problem stands fittingly at the end of the development of the equestrian figure in an all-round aspect, a development that began in the highly intellectual art of the Renaissance with Verrocchio and Leonardo.

The difficulties encountered by the sculptor of the equestrian statue are partly due to the unnatural position into which the horse is forced by the rider and which results in an unplastic and complicated position of the legs. The flexing of the head by the reins, the slow, collected walk are unnatural to the horse. A horse walks naturally with neck outstretched, with irregular steps, often standing still with head bent down. Man, trying to improve upon nature, adds to his own difficulties, changing what could be a simple task into an almost insurmountable one. That an unbridled horse in a natural, undramatic aspect can be conceived as a perfect model for a sculpture in the round has been shown by Gerhard Marcks in his bronze statuette (Fig. 95). This German artist belongs — like Maillol and Despiau in France — to those sculptors who, in a reaction against the complicated compositions, open forms and impressionistic technique of the age of Rodin, strive for classical simplicity, for an expression of lyrical intimacy and for a compact and smooth treatment of forms. Their poetic realism, adapted generally to the traditional motifs of draped and undraped human figures, lives on in a world which has been revolutionized by mechanization and by a belief in abstract conceptions. Yet, it cannot be denied that they give us as much pleasure as more advanced sculptors, reminding us of the fact that we are quite able to enjoy in fifteenth-century Florentine art paintings by Masolino and Fra Angelico as much as the progressive works of Masaccio and Uccello. And these sculptors are not untouched by the ideas of our time; this is proved by the delight they take in a return to idyllic nature, for which the horse statuette here reproduced may serve as example. It also demonstrates that these sculptors know how to make occasional use of the experiences of the age they defied. The perforated construction of the bronze animal could, from a formal point of view, be imagined only as a result of the development of the open-form sculpture of the Baroque period and of Rodin.

The problem of the open spaces between the legs is in Marcks' horse solved with the greatest simplicity by rendering the horse grazing with head hanging down: the head connects the torso with the ground and thus adds solider form to the legs supporting the body; together with the hind legs, it acts at the same time as a complete frame around the open spaces, which are arranged in a perfect pattern. The space between neck and left front leg corresponds in reverse to the one between the forward-stepping right front leg and the left hind leg. Similarly, the high open angles between each of the front and each of the hind legs correspond to each other. Unfortunately, the photograph does not give the plastic value created within this framework by the turn of the head to the front and the placing of the right front leg forward at an angle. It is as if we were looking into an open hut or cave encased by a heavy roof and by a carefully designed lattice-work. Other views of the horse give similarly satisfying aspects, for it is a piece of sculpture made to be seen from all sides.

Sculptors of abstract tendency took up the problem of the horse without rider as early as the beginning of the cubistic movement. Two French sculptors who died at an early age during the first World War, Gaudier-Brzeska and Duchamp-Villon, were, about 1914, concerned with representing the horse in an abstract manner, giving it at the same time volume and elasticity. Only sketches of Gaudier-Brzeska's ideas (Fig. 96) have been preserved, but they show progressively an increasing balance of the different sections of the horse's body in simplified curves. Duchamp-Villon created in his bronze (Fig. 97) an expressive symbol of a horse, half animal, half machine. He translated the idea of "horsepower" into volume filled with explosive energy and combined the mechanical sense of our time with an understanding of the functions of nature.

An attempt at synthesis of an abstract and a realistic style, which some sculptors at present try to achieve, is the effective construction of a fantastic horse executed by Mary Callery (Fig. 98). With the boldness of the prehistoric sculptors, the artist has changed the object of nature in accordance with sculptural principles. Treated almost like a wire sculpture, the head and feet of the horse are enormously elongated, while the body is reduced to a narrow central part, out of which the extremities jump forward, spoutlike. The neck of the horse rises from the center like a fountain whose water masses in the returning fall leave a clearly conceived space in the middle. The creation of this center volume produced by the framework of the legs, and apparently moving upward from a rising ground towards the neck, is the essential formal element of the sculpture. The exaggerated elongation of the extremities is justified to some degree through the character and behavior of the wildly charging and screaming animal. Although the inner life force expressed in this fashion is not quite as convincing as that of Picasso's shattered horses in *Guernica,* from which the present sculpture is derived, we see here clearly in which direction modern sculpture of this type tends, towards a goal of equal intensity in formal and in spiritual qualities.

Chapter VII

Sculpture in the Round in Prehistoric and Modern Times

Part I

In Chapter V we mentioned that most sculpture of historical periods is relief sculpture and that only two historical epochs in European art — the late Greek and Roman and again the post-Renaissance periods — produced a type of sculpture that was intended to be seen from all sides. Purposely, there has been no reference to the all-round sculpture which existed in the prehistoric epochs. Discussion of this type of plastic art has been reserved for a special chapter, because it should be considered in connection with certain far-reaching tendencies of a similar kind in contemporary sculpture.

In prehistoric times the earth was still empty and bare. Vast spaces of land and water were without human beings. Man was nearer to earth and to heaven. His dwellings were in the ground or among rocks, in caves not visible from the outside, not changing the circumstances of nature. When man wanted to erect monuments to his gods or to his heroes, these would not be designed in connection with architecture, for there was no architecture. The monuments might rise out of thick forests in tropical countries and adapt themselves to their wild and entangled surroundings, as in India, or might be placed in wide-open spaces, as in Europe, where they could be seen from all sides. Their character was always one with nature: mounds of earth or heavy stones served as altars or tombs, large rocks erected like pillars became symbols for cults and memorials. Since the forms of these sculptures were abstract, they provided varying excellent views from many angles, like all free-standing abstract sculpture.

Example from the Old Testament

From parts of the Old Testament that go back to the fourth and third millenniums B.C., we learn what symbolic meaning these primitive structures of stone could have. Laban and Jacob erected a heavy stone to seal a covenant between them (*Genesis* 31: 43–54): "And Laban said unto Jacob, Now therefore come thou, let us make a covenant, I and thou; and let it be for a witness between me and thee. And Jacob took a stone, and set it up for a pillar. And Jacob said unto his brethren, Gather stones; and they took stones, and made an heap; and they did eat there upon the heap. . . . And Laban said to Jacob, Behold this heap, and behold this pillar, which I have cast betwixt me and thee; This heap be witness, and this pillar be witness, that I will not pass over this heap to thee, and that thou shalt not pass over this heap and this pillar unto me, for harm. . . . Then Jacob offered sacrifice upon the mount, and called his brethren to eat bread; and they did eat bread, and tarried all night in the mount."

Only a people living very close to nature and regarding her as sacred in all her creations could give such deep symbolic meaning to a stone and a pillar.

We find the same symbolism expressed in simple prehistoric structures in the northern part of Europe. Large single rocks of pillar shape or whole series of stones arranged in avenues or in a circle were erected in memory of great events or for cult purposes by the early Germanic tribes; and large heaps of stones or cairns were piled up above the dead bodies of their leaders. Best known are the menhirs of Brittany (Figs. 99 and 100) and Stonehenge in England; similar constructions existed in Spain and Portugal, in Holland, Germany and Scandinavia. When such constructions were also discovered in North Africa, Syria and Southern Russia, they were thought to mark the route which the Indo-Germanic peoples took from Central Asia to Europe. But this theory has been abandoned; it is more likely that wherever these structures appear they reveal the extent of the Teutonic tribes in Europe and beyond, at certain stages of their wanderings.

How long the old Germanic custom of piling up heaps of stone over the bodies of their heroes lasted may be seen from Dante's *Divine Comedy*. In the "Purgatorio" (Canto III), the poet meets the last of the Hohenstaufen kings, Manfred, who was killed in the battle of Benevento (1266). Dante is deeply moved when Manfred tells the story of his burial near the battlefield under a huge cairn, which was erected by the soldiers of his army, each contributing a stone. But the body was disinterred by order of the Pope and deposited on the banks of the Verde outside the boundaries of the Papal states.

> Yet at the bridge's head my bones had lain
> Near Benevento, by the heavy mole
> Protected; but the rain now drenches them,
> And the wind drives, out of the kingdom's bounds,
> Far as the stream of Verde, where, with lights
> Extinguish'd, he removed them from their bed.
> Yet by their curse we are not so destroyed
> But that the eternal love may turn, while hope
> Retains her verdant blossom . . .[1]

This occurred at a time when mediaeval architecture was at its height, when kings were buried in cathedrals. But Manfred had been excommunicated, and his army, far away from home after the defeat, had no time to find a burial place. His warriors suddenly remembered the old

1. Dante, *Divine Comedy*, translated by Henry Francis Cary, 1814.

custom of their ancestors of many centuries past and, just as they had done, honored their leader by covering him with a cairn that could be seen from far away.

Memories of man's childhood live forever in the subconsciousness of later generations. Measured by the vastness of prehistoric epochs, the interval between our own day and the beginning of time is not much greater than that from the thirteenth century back to those earliest ages. These memories, slumbering quietly in us so long as advanced civilization satisfies our wishes for outer happiness, disturb our dreams when the present is too much opposed to the natural state from which we started. When we are shut in by narrow city streets, we long for the immense spaces which embraced our earliest life. When cities become insecure in war and threaten to bury us under a terrible collapse of buildings, we long for the security which nature provided for us even in the most primitive stages, when an inimical animal world surrounded us. No animal's fury can be compared to the infernal machinery of destruction invented by man. Cities, once so secure, have failed to be indestructible; not so nature. Nature is always there, waiting for the return of the Prodigal Son who believed that he could live without the house whence he came.

Monuments to the dead
When we now think of indestructible monuments dedicated to an eternal spirit or to the immortals among men, we no longer imagine them within the walls and streets of cities, but in a primeval and heroic landscape, where men once lived before architecture was invented.

Often the question is raised as to what kind of monuments we want to have erected for the dead of the second World War. No one would like a repetition of the badly conceived, realistic bronze statues of fighting soldiers or victory angels produced after the first World War and now encountered on squares in hundreds of cities, big and small, everywhere in Europe and America. We cannot now imagine those who have been killed in the wars as individuals in uniform, or as representatives of a joyous victory — for victory is given to no one on earth — but as innocent human beings whose tragic fate has driven them for unknown causes prematurely to death. We cannot forget them, not so much because they were sacrificed for their country, but because we loved them. We want to remember, not their fighting, but their human spirit; and we want to give the expression of that spirit as wide a space as possible, so that later generations may be impressed by its vastness. When we have found in nature a solitary place with great spaces around it, there we may have a serious grave monument of symbolic character, erected as a tumulus or stone structure of simple outline whence avenues may radiate, lined with plastic abstract forms which prepare for the arrival of the living. Such a memorial will be monumental in character, for it will comprise a huge expanse of space and fill it with a strong elementary pattern of original design. It will be at the same time majestic and intimate, for the mount will point down to earth where the dead were buried and up to heaven where they now exist. In such places the spirits of the dead may dwell lightly between heaven and earth and carry the mind of the living into their own infinite realm.

It may be said that such monuments are without tradition in our Western world. It is true that they do not correspond to the ideas in cemeteries of recent centuries, but they are not without tradition in the history of mankind as a whole, if we remember the recurrent waves in which they appear again and again from prehistoric times on. To those structures of the early Germanic tribes already mentioned let us add those of mediaeval China, which perhaps more than any yet existing may serve as examples for memorial tombs corresponding to the ideas of our time (Figs. 101, 102). Not that they should be imitated literally; but it is possible to imagine that modern monuments could be conceived in a similar spirit. The Ming tombs outside of Peking are well known, with their splendid avenues of sculptures leading towards a tumulus seen from afar. These sculptures consist of priests and animals — elephants and lions — forming a cortège in the funeral procession (Fig. 101). But more beautiful and even more modern in spirit, because of their less realistic treatment of the sculptural parts, are the tombs of the T'ang dynasty discovered by the French mission, Segalen–de Voisins–Lartigue. We reproduce a tomb of Emperor T'ang Kao-tsong (683 A.D.), which shows that the abstract formations of tumuli and rocks play here a greater part in the whole than they do in the later tombs (Fig. 102).

Henry Moore

There is evidence that our time is well aware of the ideas underlying these monuments of symphonic sculpture and has developed similar tendencies in a new and original form, proven by the work of the remarkable English sculptor, Henry Moore. More than any other contemporary sculptor, he expresses our deep longing for a closer connection with the elemental forces of nature as found in primeval deserts, mountains and forests, away from cities, away from artificial life guided by intellect instead of by emotional energies. Other modern sculptors like Arp, Vantongerloo, Brancusi, Zadkine, Lipchitz preceded Moore in creating abstract sculpture intended to be placed out of doors, but their accomplishments depended more upon the inventions of the Machine Age and the highly evolved life of cities than do Moore's, who conjures up the spirit of wild, uninhabited nature in a manner never to be found in other sculptures of recent times.

Moore's art may seem unexpected in a country which has not produced great sculptors for more than four hundred years; but if one recalls the strength of pagan sculpture in the earliest European periods and again in the Norman art of mediaeval England, we can well understand that such a tradition had to come to life again after an interval, like a stream that flows continually under the ground but comes to the surface when an earthquake causes a sudden break in the earth's crust. This "break" occurred in England when the world wars brought about a complete change in social conditions. Insecurity on this island, which had been a haven of security throughout its history, was increased by bombings which drove city people into the country and into shelters.

Hertiage

Moore is one of the few artists who have turned war experiences to artistic creation. When, in his powerful drawings he represents people living in shelters (Fig. 103) or miners working in caves, we do not feel that he renders a specific passing event of modern war, as most war painters seek to do; we find that he adds an eternal character to these life studies, which takes them out of the atmosphere of momentary happenings. The figures rolled up in blankets, lying in endless rows in tunnels, have, with their small heads and enormous bodies, something supernatural about them. They appear like ghosts of the earth, as if they had lived for eternities under the ground of which they are a part. Their connection with the protecting earth around them is complete.

The War

The same spirit penetrates his out-of-door sculptures, some of which are almost abstract, with only a slight suggestion of human form. There is, for instance, a stone composition similar to a cube (Fig. 104), but of irregular shape, presenting new, unexpected views to different sides. It rests upon a heavy stone pillar of the type we see at Stonehenge. While the pillar is nature untouched, the form at the top is nature filled with the energy emanating from an artist's mind; clear-cut planes change into rounded outlines; the forms break apart suddenly whenever the eye tires of one aspect, all in accordance with the strong directing will of the artist. It is as if organic life entered for the first time an inorganic form and created a revolt in movements of different direction.

In another sculpture, the whole pillar has taken on the semblance of a human figure: a mother holding a child in her arms (Fig. 105). With a strange look the figures stare, half awake, into the far distance as if they were guarding the sacred aspect of a barren landscape against the intru-

141

sion of man.

Most impressive are some reclining figures, half rock, half human being, with huge, expanding limbs and small, indefinite heads (Figs. 106, 107). The rock is weathered and hollowed through age, but subconscious life is awakening in the shattered forms and makes them grow like the trees around them. It is as if we were witnessing the transition from earth to life and, at the same time, the transition from life to decay. These double transformations give to the forms something as ageless as nature itself.

Moore's drawings suggest how he intends to have such statues placed (Fig. 108). In a wide, desert-like landscape two irregularly shaped pillars of red stone stand erect; the silhouettes of the inner sides are related to one another in a corresponding rhythm. The hugeness of these works can be judged by a comparison with two minute human figures to be discerned in the distance. In front rests one of the wooden figures, as if in a subconscious dream, the long limbs stretched out as if soon to awaken to life. A timeless atmosphere pervades both figures and landscape.

In another drawing (Fig. 109), we see pillar-shaped, abstract stone statues like pagan images standing in a valley and on promontories in a rugged, hilly landscape where no trees or plants grow. They are like remnants of the free and wild life of a people who prayed to the gods of nature. In curious contrast, there appear in the distance porticoes from two Greek temples of white marble. But the somber tokens of heathen belief are stronger than the light, symmetrical, classical construction; they are parts of nature, expressions of primitive people full of faith, whose minds are not yet disturbed by the mathematical calculations which created the temples. By intensifying his intellect, man separated himself from intimate connection with the earth and lost his natural strength.

Part 2

Relation of primitive man to the animal world

Primitive man had a much closer relationship to the animal world than we. Endowed with clearer instincts than civilized man, who is guided mainly by intellect, he understood better the spirit of animals, who also are guided solely by instinct. Whether friends or enemies, animals were a constant source of interest; they seemed to primitive man in many ways like himself, yet they were mysteriously separated from him by other qualities. The earliest sculptures and paintings of animals are more alive than those of human figures.

Probably the first animals to be represented in art were those with which primitive man could live in peace and with which he could work, such as horses, cattle, sheep, dogs, cats. Next to be represented were those that were his enemies and excited his fear. But there were other animals, neither friendly nor inimical, that lived their detached life, in the earth like reptiles, in the water like fish, in the air like birds. To these animals primitive people attached magic traits, because they seemed to have little in common with man except that they lived amid the same basic elements of earth, water, air. These animals were more closely connected with the elements than man himself, having developed certain qualities superior to those of man. Hence they deserved to be venerated and were considered to have reached a stage only attainable by man after death. Such creatures as turtles, toads, snakes, cicadas, fish and birds were parts of the cosmogonic ideas of most primitive races and were represented usually as symbols of the resurrection, this being suggested by their transformation from one stage of existence to another.

Primitive animal sculpture in the round   The representation of these animals in sculpture was, like all primitive sculpture, visualized in the round, since they were studied in wild nature without the background of architecture. It so happened that the bodily forms of these creatures were well adapted to being modeled in the round: at least this applies to the reptiles like snakes, turtles, toads, frogs and dragons, the dragon being an imagined combination of different types of reptiles. The snake when circularly coiled at rest or preparing to strike provided a splendid model for an all-round piece of sculpture, as we see in frequent examples of early Mexican art (Fig. 110). Toads and frogs can easily be fitted into an almost square cubic form, since their legs are closely attached to their bodies; while the turtle has the shape of a tumulus sloping down evenly on all sides, from which head and legs only slightly protrude (Figs. 111, 112). The dragon too can be bent with ease into a circular composition, as Flannagan's fine field-stone composition shows (Fig. 113).

We should mention in this connection the sacred beetle (scarab) (Fig. 114) which was venerated in Egypt for similar reasons as the toad and turtle in China. It symbolized life and life after death, as it lived an existence both in and out of the earth, one of constant change. The scarab — although belonging to a different type of organic creature — had in common with the toad and turtle, the quality of lending itself easily to sculpture in the round.

The case was somewhat different with creatures such as the cicada, a favorite subject in early Chinese bronzes and again in Western art during the migration period[2] because of the many stages in the development of this insect, from the egg to the larva, the pupa, the mature locust — a development which seemed to Chinese philosophers mysteriously related to the metempsychosis of man. We find it represented frequently in its earlier stages, and in its finished stage with large transparent wings as ornament in relief sculpture, but never in all-round plastic forms. The reason for this is probably the same as that which prevented primitive people from representing fish and birds in any other form than painting or relief sculpture: they were unable to express in all-round sculpture the essential characteristic of these creatures, swift movement in air or water. Only contemporary sculptors have succeeded in such representations, and they only by means unknown to primitive artists.

Snakes, dragons, turtles and toads are related to one another in early Chinese mythology.[3] Two snake-dragons created the Great Flood by spitting out the water that filled their bodies; once emptied, they were changed into turtles, the demons of the earth. In the Han period the turtle combined with the snake symbolized the darkness out of which new life was created. For this reason the turtle represents fertility, as does the toad. In early bronzes a toad sometimes appears between a woman's legs, as a sign of fertility. According to an early Chinese source, the turtle, like woman, is influenced by the moon, increasing and decreasing every month. A woman once stole the herb of immortality from the gods and escaped with it to the moon, where she was changed into a turtle; her silhouette can still be seen in the dark spots of the full moon. Sometimes in Chinese legends a toad is the symbol of the moon, while in East Indian legends the goddess of fertility is accompanied by a toad or a frog.

In Mexican and Central American mediaeval cultures, toad, turtle and snake play an important part in religion and mythology. Tlaltecuhtli, Lord of the Earth, had as attributes a toad and an alligator. But better known is Quetzalcoatl, the feathered serpent, God of Learning, of Time and of the Year; several of the temples dedicated to him were of cylindrical shape and rested on square or cylindrical platforms, the buildings suggesting the round body of the snake, the entrance, its open mouth.[4] Here we are dealing with an art already remote from prehistoric times, but certainly based upon the same very early conceptions. In this instance is shown how a type of architecture with an all-round aspect was derived from a primitive form of sculpture in the round. To the finest all-round

2. Herbert Kühn, in "Ipek," 1925.
3. C. Hentze, *Frühchinesische Bronzen und Kultdarstellungen,* Antwerp, 1935; M. Rostovtzeff, *The Animal Style in South Russia and China,* 1929.
4. George C. Vaillant, *Aztecs of Mexico;* 1941, pp. 160–180.

sculptures in Mexican art belong the altar of coiled serpents like that in the Mexican National Museum (Fig. 110). The Aztec sculptors have also produced beautiful all-round small sculptures of compact forms, executed in jade or other costly stones.

Among the oldest sculptures in the round in China are representations of toads and turtles in small and monumental stone compositions. Examples of both creatures in plastic art have been found in the royal tombs of An-Yang, which can be dated about 1200 B.C. (Figs. 111, 112). Their symbolic meaning is expressed by the ornaments upon their backs and by the ferocity given to the ugly faces of these demons of the earth. A later representation of a large turtle, from a funeral avenue leading to a tomb of the year 518 A.D., shows a more realistic conception, but retains the all-round aspect in a composition of monumental force in which a stele with decorations on all sides is carried by that strong animal (Fig. 115).

Modern animal sculpture in the round

It is not chance, but a direct result of our longing for a better comprehension of the innermost forces of nature, that our interest in the primitive sculptures of these earthbound creatures has been awakened and that modern sculpture has again taken up their representation. The most expressive are those by John Flannagan (Fig. 116). How far away we are here from nineteenth-century conceptions! Who could then have imagined a large frog or a coiled snake as a fit subject for an independent piece of sculpture? These works by Flannagan are undoubtedly influenced by sculptures of very early periods, of the type we have described. But the fact that they are, in spite of this, completely original, and also that they have found a public that considers them to express its own ideas, proves how much more direct our relationship to life in nature and its influence upon men has become since the end of the nineteenth century. The fact that Flannagan has more than one serious follower among contemporary American sculptors in the rendering of these mysterious animals further reveals a connection between this sculpture and the spiritual conceptions of our time. A California sculptress, Pegot Waring, has done several stone sculptures of simplified forms, representing strange animals of prehistoric appearance; a large snakelike reptile with blown-up flanks and trembling tail (Fig. 117), and a water animal, half whale, half fish (Fig. 118), both excellent sculptures conceived in the round. The fish can be easily turned off-center on a point below the belly, thus reminding us of Brancusi's *Miracle* in the Museum of Modern Art in New York.

Brancusi and Calder

Brancusi has placed this piece of white polished marble, cut in the shape of an upright, sitting seal, upon a round pedestal, which is set in slow motion by a motor, thus presenting the sculpture from all sides. In this work — as in many of Calder's plastic compositions — movement is expressed with the help of actual motion, an idea that could occur only to artists living in a time when extraordinary problems of fast motion have been solved through the production of machines that carry man rapidly over land, through water and through air. These inventions have made us conscious, more than ever before, of motion in space; but at the same time they have made us conscious of the instability of the ground upon which we live, so that we have a feeling of insecurity which we can overcome only by developing to a high degree the sense of balance which nature has given us.

Nature's organic equivalents to the mechanical devices invented by man for flying are fish and birds. With our new understanding of motion in air and water, the representation of these creatures in sculpture has entered a new stage of development. Flannagan created a whale as a separate piece of sculpture, although connecting it with a traditional story from the Bible, that of Jonah (Fig. 119, bronze version reproduced). The large bluish piece of field stone, whose shape when he found it reminded Flannagan of a whale, has hardly been changed in contour by the artist. It is placed upon one narrow end, as if the whale were standing on its head, thus giving us the feeling of an unstable yet balanced position in the midst of the insecure element of water.

Flannagan's art is born out of nature and has little to do with the Machine Age. Neither Brancusi nor Calder, however, could be imagined without its accomplishments, although each proceeds in a very different manner to produce movement. It is true that they both strive for simplified forms, as all original artists of our time do; and both go back to nature as the first source of their art; but the highly developed civilized mind is very evident in the precision they give to the execution of their work and in the mathematical balance they apply to their compositions. Calder's whale (Fig. 120) likewise stands upon its head, balanced upon curved fins; but this whale seems to be filled with the power that makes it spout water high into the air and seems to be fighting with sharp-edged fins against surrounding enemies. It is made of sheet steel, that is, of a material produced by a very advanced civilization, while Flannagan's sculpture could almost have been formed with simple prehistoric instruments. The beauty of Calder's work lies in the energy of his lines, which can be produced only with the sharpness of cut steel, and in its spatial development, which goes further than Flannagan's, since it expands more decisively into all dimensions.

Brancusi and Calder, also, have created abstract sculptures of fish;

Brancusi in an individual piece executed in two variations, one in marble (Fig. 121), one in polished metal; Calder in a mobile called *Steel Fish* (Fig. 122) in which the fish is set in actual motion by being attached to a delicately balanced skeleton of rods and iron plates. The simplified form of the fish is, in both instances, almost the same, yet the illusion of swift motion created varies considerably according to the different characters of the two artists. Brancusi is content to use the individual closed form of the object, for he belongs to the type of sculptor who loves compact volume above everything; but he gives to the marble fish, by a wonderfully polished surface, a remarkable transparency and airiness, and to the metal fish a shimmering shininess, so that in both instances the material has lost all heaviness. Stone has become fluid, as if light were shining through it, metal, like glittering scales upon which the sun is reflected. The suggestion of the form of the fish with a sharp pointed mouth and a blunt tail is, then, sufficient to produce the effect of a fast moving creature, whose vibrant individual life is expressed in the unevenness of the outlines above and below the body and in its off-center balance.

In Calder's case the shape of the fish is part of a carefully balanced machinery, which consists mostly of virtual volume, that is, the dissolved parts of the composition are at least as important as the solid ones. The fish, which is actually moving, seems, so to speak, in its element, as it is surrounded by lighter forms of thin, elongated or round bodies which we could well imagine to be moving nearer or further through the water around it. We are, at the same time, made aware that the shape of the fish in this case, as in Brancusi's, is similar to fast moving mechanical objects invented in our time, like dirigibles or torpedoes, a fact which increases for us the illusion of movement.

The representation of birds in flight sculptured in the round was for primitive man as impossible as the representation of fish in motion. Some kind of attempt to portray flight was made by the American Indians in their effigies on mounts, some of which reproduce birds. One of these effigies on a mount in Madison, Wisconsin, has the shape of a seagull with spread wings, the width of the wings extending to fifty-two feet. It is true that these effigies covering the top of the mounts in a raised pattern are really relief sculptures, but as they are seen from above and can be appreciated equally well from all sides, they have somewhat the character of all-round sculptures. In this case the illusion of a bird in flight is, indeed, produced to some degree if we stand in the center of the mount, where we have the feeling of being carried on the back of the bird down towards the lake as the goal of flight.

147

What Brancusi, however, has created in his rightly famous sculpture *Bird in Space* (Fig. 123) is of a much more direct and stimulating appeal, although it in no way represents a realistic image of a bird. Its effect is based upon form and material that are products of highly developed modern technics. It is a question whether the imagination of people of any other age than ours would find this sculpture so exciting, because it is only through modern inventions in the field of flying machines that we have become accustomed to thinking of certain forms as expressive of the idea of fast motion. It has even been said that Brancusi in his *Bird in Space* unknowingly produced the shape of a propeller, which was later found to be the most practical shape for use in aeroplanes. However, it must be said that when Brancusi's work was placed next to such a propeller, in an exhibition at the Museum of Modern Art, the likeness was found to be only superficial and unessential. The *Bird in Space,* in its irregular shape and unexpected light reflections, seemed a product of nature like all art creations, while the propeller appeared to be a mechanical product made only for practical use.

In this chapter, the theme of the sculptures representing earth, water and air-bound animals has been stressed as much as their form. If we were speaking only of abstract art, it might be said that this was superfluous. Knowledge of literary content is in fact not essential to the enjoyment of art, but it does help to release the imagination towards a greater understanding. And besides, it is a revelation of the spirit of the artist and of the time in which his work is produced.

Chapter VIII

Sculpture and Religion

Part I

The sculptor's task in the formation of religions

The law that Moses gave to his people, about 1500 B.C., prohibiting images of God, was not accepted by mankind. The Second Commandment says: "Thou shalt not make unto thee any graven image, or any likeness of any thing that is in heaven above, or that is in the earth beneath, or that is in the water under the earth." Nevertheless, people from Moses' day to ours have made images representing their gods, in every imaginable form; the form has been taken from creatures living on earth, under the earth or in the water.

Religion does not seem possible without image-making: we cannot pray to something that has no form. And this form necessarily takes on the likeness of ourselves or of other living creatures. That works of art influence the nature of the image in the mind of the worshiper, we have seen from Leonardo's Christ in *The Last Supper* and Michelangelo's Madonna in the *Pietà* of St. Peter's. But such vague associations in the educated mind are not sufficient for the simple man, who wants to have the image in front of him so that he can address it as another person.

Primitive man wants to have the image in his hand, and, as we have noted, this was one of the reasons why the beginning of all arts was plastic art. Primitive man treats an image as one of his companions who has power over nature; his prayer is like a friendly admonition. If the prayer is not successful, the god is maltreated.

It is a step further in the development of mankind when the image is placed reverently above the worshiper, so that he can kneel in prayer before it. God is no longer a companion, but a power living in a higher sphere.

Even so, the pious still like to imagine the form of their god in as life-like a way as possible. Thus, it was not difficult for the rulers of primitive races to make their subjects believe that they, the rulers, were gods to whom men ought to pray. We find this form of theocratic hierarchy not only among African and Polynesian tribes but among such highly civilized peoples as the Assyrians, Babylonians and Egyptians.

Whether religion is a purely spiritual one, founded by a reformer like Buddha or Christ, or whether it partakes of absolute, worldly power, the artist will always have a great deal to say with regard to the conception of sacred images. And it is important to realize that this artist, not only in remote times, but as long as religion has held sway, is principally the sculptor. It is well known that in early Asiatic empires and in Egypt the gods were represented in sculpture and never in painting. But it is less known that the Greeks too could only imagine their religious exercises taking place in front of a full plastic figure (Fig. 124), not before a relief or a painting. Reliefs and paintings (vase paintings, for instance) were reserved for worldly representations, as in Egyptian and Cretan art.

All this means that the sculptor has had a lasting influence upon the formation of religion. He does not actually create it, but the origin of religion is so closely connected with the sculptor's work that we may well ask whether religion would be possible without the plastic arts. We could not imagine Buddhism without the Buddha statues fashioned according to the idea sculptors conceived of the founder. It is also difficult to imagine the Christian religion without the portraits of Christ that were invented by the early Christian sculptors. In this case, we can still trace the manner in which the now generally accepted type of Christ came to life under the artists' hands. No one knew how Christ had looked, by the time, two or three centuries after his death, his religion was beginning to conquer the world; the sculptors therefore depicted him as the Apollo of the Romans, round-headed, youthful and without a beard. Later, when Constantinople became the center of Christianity in the East, the artists could not imagine a dignified person without a beard of the shape worn by Byzantine emperors, and they gave Christ the fine narrow features, elongated by the dark, pointed beard that was the fashion at the Byzantine court. The Romanesque and Gothic sculptors bequeathed this type to the Renaissance, but each period made changes in the representation of Christ in accordance with its own ideas of beauty and spirituality.

Sculptors, therefore, whenever they created religious images, unconsciously forced their own ideas upon the worshiping masses. Of course, when asked by the priesthood to make images of God, they were instructed to embody in these works certain religious ideas. Yet, since a work of art is never completely preconceived, but grows in form and content while the artist is creating it, the likenesses of God in the artist's work were as much a part of his own ideas as of the priests' who commissioned them. In fact, the more the sculptor succeeded in creating a living masterpiece, the greater would be his influence upon the pious, who prayed to what was mostly the artist's own conception. Thus, we may say that Phidias, in creating the Athena Parthenos and the Zeus at Olympia, did as much to establish Greek religion as Homer who, Herodotus says, created the Greek gods. Without the imagination of the artist, whether poet or sculptor, the formation of a religion cannot be conceived. The Greek idea was that art belonged to the gods, not to men; therefore, all

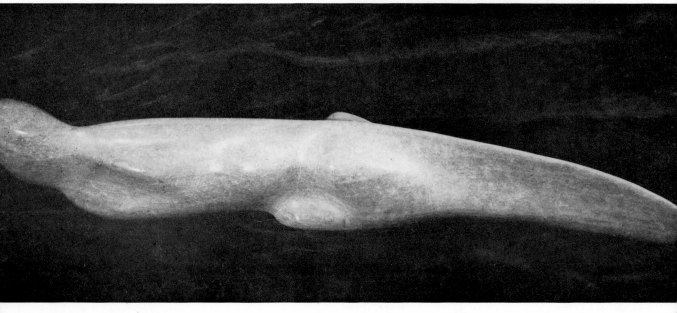

116. *J. B. Flannagan*

117. *P. Waring*

118. *P. Waring*

153

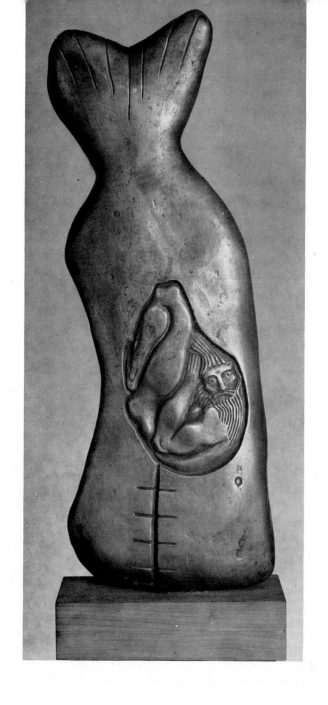

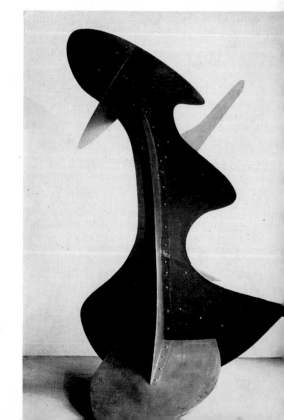

119. *J. B. Flannagan*
120. *A. Calder*

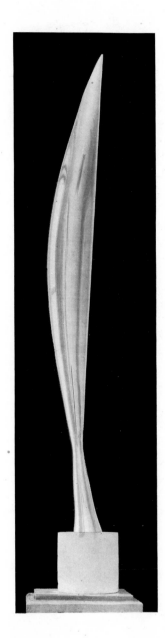

121, 123. *C. Brancusi*

122. *A. Calder*

124. *Greek, 5th century* B.C.

125. *French, 12th century*

126. *English, 15th century*

127. *P. Legros*

128. *A. Modigliani*

129. *K. Schmidt-Rottluff*

130. *Aztec*

131. *Central American*

132. *G. Kolbe*
133. *E. Barlach*

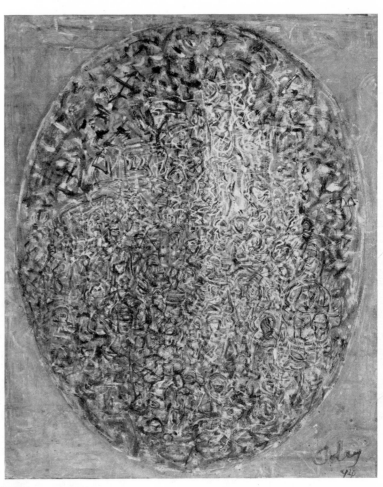

134. *M. Tobey*

135. *M. Graves*

136. *C. Brancusi*

137. *J. B. Flannagan*

139. *A. Calder*

138. *J. B. Flannagan*

art was religion. But even if in other early cultures this thought was not as clearly formulated as by the philosophic Greek mind, it remains true that the sculptors, those anonymous artists of primitive tribes, substantially aided the founders of religion by perpetuating their ideas and transforming them into reality.

Part 2

Painting rivaling sculpture after the Renaissance

The relationship of Leonardo and Michelangelo to the art of sculpture shows how much the conception of the artist in regard to religion changed during the Renaissance. Leonardo's works in sculpture — portraits and equestrian statues — have no connection with mediaeval religious sculpture. He reveals himself as the great individualist he was, in his lack of any interest in the original purpose of sculpture — its service to religion.

Michelangelo, on the other hand, created some of the most moving religious sculptures, but even in these works we feel that his religiousness has not the directness and complete absence of self of the primitive sculptor. He cannot subdue his own strong individuality in dealing with a religious subject, but must impose it upon even the most exalted representation. Though longing to participate in the religious revival of the Counter-Reformation, Michelangelo was unable to abandon his relations with the humanistic world around him. His split personality resulted in the tragic content of his religious art, in the tortured expression of all his figures who, while yearning for spirituality, cannot renounce the sensuality which is the source of their strength.

That Leonardo believed in the superiority of painting signifies that, in his day, painting was successfully rivaling sculpture. It is characteristic that Michelangelo, who was a born sculptor and who called painting a work for women and sluggards, was forced to devote half of his time to painting because his greatest patrons preferred it to sculpture.

From the fifteenth century on, until our time, sculpture increasingly lost the all-powerful importance it possessed in primitive epochs, in Greece and in the Middle Ages. Painting took its place, attracting the interest of the masses by developing new fields of subject-matter which were not suitable for sculpture, such as historical, genre and landscape representation. In certain periods and in certain countries, painting led the figurative arts to such an extent that sculpture was almost forgotten; this was so, for instance, in Dutch and Flemish art of the sixteenth and seventeenth centuries, in Spanish and English art of the seventeenth and eighteenth centuries. Painters like Bosch and Bruegel, like Rubens and Rembrandt, like Greco and Velasquez, like Hogarth and Reynolds, are known to everyone, but who knows even by name any sculptors of their respective countries during these periods?

It is the overwhelming influence of painting, since the sixteenth century, that has resulted in modern times in the public's preference for painting rather than sculpture. In helping to build up a well-balanced museum collection, I was told repeatedly, by those in a position to know the trend of the general public, that it would be better to buy paintings than sculpture, because the former was more popular, that, in the mind of people nowadays art was synonymous with painting. Such a point of view would have been impossible in times when religious art was dominant and sculpture was the expression of this art. And I do not doubt that in the future the balance will again be in favor of sculpture, if art will have become again, as in the most distant past, the source of spirituality and religion.

The preference of the public for paintings, at present, is revealed in the exaggerated and unjustified appreciation of sculptures which are seen through the painter's eye or are actually executed by painters. From Daumier on to Renoir and Degas and further to Picasso and Matisse, painters have occasionally worked in sculpture in connection with their problems in painting, as some of the older masters, like Dürer, Poussin or Rubens, also did. These sculptures are interesting only from a biographical point of view, in the study of the art of these painters; they have added nothing to the fundamental problems of sculpture; they lack the necessary expression of volume filled with energy — this applies, for instance, to Renoir's boneless sculptures — and have (a characteristic of sculptures executed by painters) very little appeal to the sense of touch.

Loss of religious content in sculpture

The absolute and monotheistic character of the Christian religion, which dominated humanity during the Middle Ages, was destroyed to a great extent by the Reformation. The individual conception of the supreme being, which the Protestant Church permitted, was followed by a movement directed against any representation of religious subjects in painting or sculpture. The destruction of sculpture by the iconoclasts of the second half of the sixteenth century was so complete that in countries like the Netherlands we are very nearly unable to reconstruct a history of mediaeval plastic art. The new concepts of religion, which retreated further and further from the original Christian dogma, found in Protestant countries an outlet almost exclusively in painting: in the mysticism of so great an individualist as Rembrandt, in the pantheism expressed in idealized landscape painting, such as the mature and grandiose compositions of Jacob Ruysdael, in the glowing and spacious views of Claude

Lorrain and Aelbert Cuyp — all of which were contemporary with the formulation of a pantheistic religion in Spinoza's philosophy. Religious church sculpture came to an end in Protestant churches after the sixteenth century.

In Catholic countries, too, the beginning of the dissolution of mediaeval Christian ideas, expressed in the Reformation, had a profound influence upon sculpture, an art which always clearly reflects the religious standards of a period. Above the altar of Romanesque or Gothic churches, the Crucified, the Madonna or the Trinity are the sole representatives of the Christian divinities (Figs. 125, 126). In Baroque altarpieces, heaven is filled with a mass of angels, saints and even donors, among whom the Madonna or Christ may assume a position, not superior, but of almost equal rank (Fig. 127). In these symphonic compositions, the figures live in open areas among clouds; increasing contrasts of light and shadow tend to dissolve the individual bodies into space.

The Deity no longer rules as powerfully and absolutely as in the Middle Ages, but shares his reign with intermediaries and permits man to include himself among his followers. He takes many different forms and thus becomes part of nature, while the mediaeval belief in the Deity meant negation of nature. This development in the Catholic Church, as illustrated in Baroque sculpture, can be compared to the pantheistic tendencies in Protestant countries; it is a trend which, after long development, should lead to the spiritual conception of space as expressed in modern abstract sculpture.

The liberation from religious dogma, characteristic of church sculpture in these periods, is still more pronounced in an entirely new field of sculpture, outside the church. The growing individualism of these ages, from the fifteenth century on, claimed the faculties of sculptors for the immortalizing of temporal heroes. Thus, we witness the (before unheard-of) development of portrait monuments in streets and in squares, in public buildings and in cemeteries, which was unknown to the Middle Ages.

The mediaeval cathedrals sometimes have tombstone and equestrian statues representing the dead in sculpture, but these tomb figures have no portrait likeness. It is significant that, until the fourteenth century, likenesses were not supposed to represent people as of more than thirty years of age, because the likeness had to be comparable with Christ's, who died at that age. The few equestrian monuments in churches are of saints or idealized kings who supported the church. This custom changed with the beginning of the Renaissance, when the tombs executed by the great

Italian sculptors represented the actual likenesses of the deceased and when the portrait statue outside the church was created to commemorate the deeds of some great military man or ruler of worldly principalities. From that time until the end of the nineteenth century, the erection of such monuments became one of the most important tasks of sculpture.

Last refuge of religion in sculpture of hero worship

Nothing better proves the purpose of sculpture as a spiritual and religious expression than the fact that, in a time of decreasing church power, it was able to live on in the last refuge of the creation of hero monuments. Hero worship was a part of the religion of the individualistic epoch. That it had, at times, even more to give to the people than the church had, is apparent in the nineteenth century, when church sculpture ceased to produce original art, yet the sculptors of monuments of pedestrian and equestrian statues of national heroes, produced, if not great, at least commendable works, satisfying the desire of the masses for the extraordinary. Not until the latter part of the nineteenth century do we find such a decrease in spiritual conception in a materialistic age that even hero worship produced works of mere empty form and unconvincing content. At the beginning of the individualistic period, monuments expressed so intensely the idea of the hero that the subjects, who would otherwise have been forgotten, live forever through such monuments as, for instance, Donatello's *Gattamelata* and Verrocchio's *Colleoni;* however, it is very doubtful whether statesmen like Lincoln, Garibaldi and Gladstone would live through the monuments erected to them, were it not that their deeds have made them unforgettable. The larger the monuments became — we think, for instance, of Gutzon Borglum's mountain portraits of American statesmen — the emptier was their content, the more miscarried their form.

The age of individualism has come to an end, and great men can no longer be immortalized by portrait statues. In a reaction against individualism, interest in portraiture has faded, and a new belief in more general ideas has taken its place. The smallest section of nature which clearly shows its connection with the cosmos and is a symbol of its eternal laws appears to us as important as man. A piece of granite from which the suggestion of the soul of an animal emerges, executed by Flannagan, has more to say to us than the mountain-sized head of Washington by Borglum.

Nineteenth-century art also gives us counter-evidence that sculpture has no right to existence if it does not deal with subjects of spiritual content. Several of the best early nineteenth-century sculptors in America followed the contemporary fashion and produced sculpture whose subjects were taken from the realm of painting, subjects illustrating contemporary novels or poems of the past, themes from ancient and modern history, or allegorical representations whose content could not be understood without the help of literary guide-books. It has been wondered why sculptors like Crawford, Brown and Greenough, who succeeded in executing good portrait statues of national heroes, failed completely in their attempts to tell stories in sculpture. Lorado Taft, after speaking in high terms of Brown's *Washington* on horseback in Union Square in New York and then calling his *Ruth* and *The Boy and Dog* undeniably absurd, says: "How it all happened is a mystery. That this amiable and intellectual but generally commonplace sculptor should have done the *Washington* of Union Square seems marvelous." The explanation consists in that, when these sculptors executed patriotic monuments, they were carried away by an exaltation of spirit communicated to them by the whole nation and comparable in intensity to religious belief; when they treated everyday themes, they had no stimulus except the group of so-called educated people who read the novels of the period. This proves clearly that the sculptor can give lasting form only to ideas that originate in a movement of the masses and not in the heads of a few privileged individuals of the upper classes.

Part **3**

Influence of primitive art on contemporary sculpture

In the origins of modern sculpture, admiration for the plastic art of primitive people like the African Negroes, the Polynesians and the pre-Columbian American Indians played an important part. The formal side of this art had a special appeal for modern painters and sculptors because in it were apparent certain organizing principles which had been lost in Western nineteenth-century sculpture. But is it possible to imitate an art of past cultures without realizing, to some degree, the content of these cultures? Hardly, unless it be in a fashion of short duration. But the movement was more than that. From 1906 to 1925 there was widespread interest in the art of primitive races, among not only artists and collectors but also the art-loving public, an interest which is still alive today. Acquisitions by art museums of examples of this art, which hitherto had been hidden away in museums of natural history, besides the formation of private collections devoted to this material, public sales, discoveries of travelers and archaeologists — all helped to spread this interest among the general public. That it affected artists and scholars was not surprising, but that it became a public vogue revealed some deeper significance. It was not accidental that the crude, and often cruel, expression of primitive art appealed greatly to a disintegrating pre-war society which, surfeited with its own products of refinement and extravagance, craved for the primitive state of man. It was in the same manner that the decadent eighteenth-century society in France, before the French Revolution, tried to find a release from over-culture in an imagined life of simplicity among the peasants.

The interest of the artists in these expressions of primitive man was undoubtedly sincere. It was not only the formal ability in the execution of these strange images that attracted them, but also the clear expression of subconscious feeling so unlike the nineteenth-century rendering of superficial external likenesses of nature based on purely intellectual conceptions. In Western art it was necessary to go far back to find an expression of such direct intensity and emotion as was found in these primitive sculptures. Even the earliest mediaeval art, in which primitive prehistoric elements of Germanic tribes are still preserved, seemed covered with a film of mellowing Christian overtones compared to what could be witnessed in African masks and wooden fetiches or in pre-Columbian American stone sculptures.

Influence upon formal conceptions

Some of the best modern French, Spanish and German painters, like Picasso, Braque, Juan Gris, Modigliani, Schmidt-Rottluff and Kirchner, began early to imitate the style of these images, and nearly all of them experimented with sculptures in wood or stone whose inspiration was directly derived from the product of the African Negroes and other primitive tribes (Figs. 128, 129). Although these imitations were well integrated into the original art of these masters, it is significant that they influenced not only form but also spirit, adding, to some degree, a somber, fearful mood unknown to these artists before. The expression of the primitive images they imitated is so powerful that anyone closely connected with them cannot help but be affected. To study them means to conjure up their demoniac powers.

The scope of the movement which developed out of the study of subconscious expression in life and art may be seen from the fact that a new science, psychoanalysis, was founded, which deals mainly with the subject of subconscious phenomena. The psychoanalysts called the desire to return to ideas of primitive imagination a regression, created in man's mind as a reaction against the subtleties of modern living. A strange longing to fall back into an earlier state of civilization seemed suddenly to capture human society.

There is no doubt that the intense preoccupation with the horrible imagery of early African and American culture carried with it a danger, the danger of releasing again the Plutonic forces of destruction which lie dormant under the surface of all highly developed civilizations.[1]

The subconscious traits exposed by primitive art gave a picture of the barbaric childhood of mankind truthful enough, yes, but dreadful to witness. The uncontrolled wildness, the unspeakable fear of primitive man was ruled by the severe, fanatical discipline of priests who demanded the complete and crushing subordination of their subjects and maintained it by the hypnotizing influence of these images. These images — the art of a people afraid and constantly threatened from all sides by enemies wishing to destroy them — appeal to the remnant of primitive man still left in each of us.

If fear is uppermost in his mind, man does not hesitate to sacrifice, in exchange for the good will and protection of his gods, whatever he thinks might be desired of him. In the desperate hope of being saved, man does not shrink from sacrificing his fellow man or torturing himself or others.

Let us remember, for instance, to what extent Aztecs and Mayas sacrificed human beings in the name of religion. Some Spanish soldiers during the conquest of Mexico counted the skulls of victims in one of the Aztec temples where these skulls were hideously exposed; there were 136,000! At the dedication of the great temple of Huitzilopochtli in 1486 the ceremony lasted several days, and prisoners, reserved for several years as the sacrificial victims, formed a procession nearly two miles long: seventy thousand were sacrificed. The power of the priesthood was based to a great extent upon the rite of human sacrifice; not even the king was able to lessen this power, as is shown by the vain efforts of one of the last Aztec kings, Nezahuacoyotl (died 1470), to stop the sanguinary rites.

As the Mayas are supposed to be more advanced in their artistic endeavors than the Aztecs, the tendency among the admirers of this civilization was to minimize as much as possible the horror of the orgies. Lately, however, archaeologists have come to the conclusion that there was not very much difference between the Mayas and Mexicans in this respect. The still existing Mayan stone altars speak too clearly: they show the ominous hollow places in which the victims were placed so that the priest could more easily cut out the heart. It does not reduce the horror of such customs to know that the Mayas' thoughts while eating the sacrificed human flesh were not quite as cannibalistic as those of the Aztecs. In the Mayan ritual the body was hurled over the steep temple sides to the waiting crowd, after the priest had cut out the heart of the still living victim and sacrificed it to the sun. The flesh was then taken home by the people

1. Henry Miller, *Sunday after the War;* 1944, p. 152.

and "eaten in a kind of communion service," while special parts, such as hands and feet, were reserved for the officiating priest. The Aztecs were, indeed, less subtle in their religious point of view and had no trouble in combining symbolic ceremonies with the pleasure of a good meal of well-dressed human flesh. According to a custom, the body of the sacrificed captive was delivered to the warrior who had captured him in battle and, after being prepared, was served by him in an entertainment for friends.

Mayan architecture and sculpture cannot be understood without a close knowledge of their religious customs. While we should be the last to criticize art from the point of view of subject-matter, we find it difficult to enjoy representations whose themes are so revolting that they force themselves unnecessarily upon the mind.

In this connection, two well-known reliefs which show Mayan and related art at its best are here reproduced. One (Fig. 130), a lintel from Yaxchilan (Menche), represents a crouching nobleman in the act of torturing himself by piercing his tongue with a rope covered with thorns: the rope is so thick and long that we wonder painfully — instead of admiring the fine execution of the relief — how he will ever be able to pull it through his tongue. The expression of the penitent is one of complete and stupid subordination to a powerful will which is represented by a priest standing over him with a vicious and demoniac face.

The other relief (Fig. 131), from Teixpan near Veracruz, is obviously not Mexican but is related to the Mayan style. The penitent in this case is not sitting, but steps forward, his face alive with excitement. He pushes a rod with a large thorn at the end through his outstretched tongue, as if it gave him the greatest pleasure. No doubt the purpose of representing such themes was to stimulate the religious to similar performances. Our minds are so confused by the perverse conception of the subject that we find it extremely difficult to enjoy its artistic value.

By a fortunate accident we happen to know more of the rites of the Aztecs and Mayas than of other half-civilized races, whose history is hidden in the tropics of Africa or the islands of the Pacific. But there can be no doubt that many of these peoples practised similar human sacrifices and self-tortures so as to conciliate their gods. And are the cruelties of the Middle Ages, of the time of the Crusades, of the Inquisition and of the French Revolution not due to the same religious fanaticism, which demanded more and more human sacrifices until those who exercised them were themselves drowned in blood?

Do we not today understand clearly, in the primitive images of human sacrifice, the spirit based on fear, the hateful fanatical spirit of war, caused by fear of the enemy and of the gods?

Primitive man sacrificed the best of its youth, decorating them and praising them as gods before they were slaughtered at the altars. Are we not now doing the same thing? Do we not send the best of our youth into battle against their will, proclaim them as heroes and let them be slaughtered for ideals of which they understand little?

Were the contemporary artists who were so enthusiastic about the religious art of uncivilized races aware of the dangerous forces hidden behind these highly aesthetic expressions? Artists always have a premonition of coming events; they well know the underlying forces of human nature. The compositions, since 1906, of Picasso and his contemporaries, under the influence of African images, stand like a threatening cloud on the horizon of Europe. We feel the rumbling under the earth preceding the breaking loose of anti-human elements in the coming wars.

Could the artists have prevented the coming catastrophe? Of course not; yet they made their influence greatly felt by pointing to the dread fascination of an art whose content propagandized suicide and human sacrifice under a tyrannical ruler. The works of art developing from these tendencies and reaching a height in Picasso's *Guernica* are undoubtedly of great importance in the modern movement, but it is debatable whether they ought to be held up as an example and inspiration to the artists of our time.

These artists, in describing the disastrous effects of the world wars, intended to condemn them; but in reality their emphasis fixes our eyes on death and destruction, thus defeating the purpose of art, which should act as a release from human misery.

Part 4

New religious spirit

New images can be created only at the inspiration of a new spirit. It is the task of the sculptor, who has in the past embodied in his work the religious spirit of his time, to help formulate the ideas which now fill the air. Signs of a new religious spirit may be observed in the work of such sculptors as Flannagan, Brancusi, Henry Moore and the sculptors of abstract compositions.

We of today can no longer be inspired by Christian or Buddhist images. In both instances, it seems to us that the spirit which inspired great religious works in the early stages of these religions has disappeared, leaving only empty repetitions of the same old formulas. The old spirit can no more be revived than can the style of the mediaeval or Baroque Christian churches or the early Buddhist temples which contained great religious works.

As for the familiar representations of Christian art, we have suddenly become more aware of the cruel, literal side of, for instance, Christ's martyrdom than of the spirit which lies behind it. In the early periods of Christian art the belief in its truth was so great that artists could ignore the unsuitableness for plastic representation of a subject like the crucifixion.

We are no longer inspired by representations of Christian martyrs, of saints whose tongues or eyes are being torn out, whose intestines are being wound upon wheels or who are flayed alive: subjects which we encounter in famous Flemish or Spanish paintings from Dirk Bouts to Rubens, from Berruguete to Ribera. Nor can we through them convey any spiritual feeling to our children. They, too, see in them only reminders of present-day war. We dislike these barbaric expressions of fanaticism, whether they occur in the art of the past or in the present, because they contradict the purity of any religious idea and forfeit the higher aims of art.

Since Oriental religions, especially Buddhism, are free from these savageries, some contemporary artists and writers have turned their eyes to the East. "It is one of the tragedies of history," says Aldous Huxley, "that Christendom should never have known anything of Buddhism beyond this garbled version of semi-legendary biography of its founder" (he is referring to a Buddhist legend which reappeared in a Christian version during the Middle Ages). "In the teachings of primitive southern Buddhism, Catholicism would have found the most salutary corrections for its strangely arbitrary theology, for its strain of primitive savagery inherited from the less desirable part of the Old Testament, for its incessant and dangerous preoccupations with torture and death, for its elaborately justified beliefs in the magic efficacy of rites and sacraments."[2]

The influence of Eastern religions has been strong since the end of the first World War upon some of the best painters and sculptors in this country and in Europe who were inclined towards mystic contemplation and resignation. We mention as examples such European sculptures of the twenties as Duchamp-Villon's bust of Baudelaire (Fig. 46), Scheibe's *Vision,* Kolbe's *Assunta* (Fig. 132) and the *Head of Angel* (Fig. 133) by Barlach, whose Slavic traits naturally directed his art towards the East. But although the artists of our time strive like the Eastern ones to express a connection with the cosmic powers, the Western mind cannot conceive life without a belief in creative activity, and only a religion that places

2. Aldous Huxley, *Grey Eminence;* 1941, p. 33.

this idea in its center is likely to give peace and happiness to our new world.

Is a religion possible without including the idea of suffering and salvation? Is not suffering the greatest incentive to religion, salvation its greatest reward? To this we must answer that the sufferings of mankind during the last decades have been so universal and indescribable that a religion that turns the mind towards happier thoughts may be a greater release to the weary spirit than one which insists on the sad realities of present-day life. Is it not better to search for ways in which nature heals the terrible wounds inflicted by war and to discover how we can participate in this healing process, than to point helplessly towards destruction or worry about our own individual sufferings?

If we can believe that the seemingly meaningless devastation of vast parts of the earth and its inhabitants is nature's endeavor to reconstruct life in a more organized and better form, we may, perhaps, arrive at a religion that praises, first of all, the creative qualities of nature as the center of life: a religion that believes in God as the creator, and in His connection with men through their creative abilities. The consciousness of this connection with Him becomes the source of the greatest human happiness, the happiness which only creative work can give man.

It is true that dissatisfaction with old religious conceptions does not mean, necessarily, that we immediately find new ones. But with the help of the artist who knows by intuition the directions of the essential thought towards which the future leads, we should be able to perceive and recognize this new conception by studying his works. By artists, we mean here not only painters, sculptors and architects, but also poets, composers of music and dance, and philosophers whose creative ability is similar to that of the artist.

New philosophy of life

Let us begin with philosophers, who ought to be the guiding spirits of the epochs, but who seldom are. As they deduce philosophic systems out of the creative ideas of each period, they are accustomed to reasoning rather than to being guided by intuition. It was, nevertheless, a philosopher, Henri Bergson — one of the great influences on the spiritual life of modern Europe — who stressed intuition as being more essential than reason, in contradiction to the tradition of French philosophy which, before Bergson's time, followed Descartes. Bergson, and with him Paul Valéry, were leaders among those who opposed the scepticism of the generation around 1900, the scepticism of such writers as Anatole France, Lemaitre and Barrès. These scepticists were a product of an age of materialism and mechanization, an age of great discoveries in all fields of science where poetic imagination had, supposedly, no right to exist. Bergson, opposing their negative attitude in spiritual matters, expressed the belief that the cause of evolution is the creative will, immanent in every form of life, which strives to conquer material forces. This creative energy binds the world together and forms the harmony in nature. God is this creative will, of which we are a part, like every other natural organism.

There is no planning in the unfolding of the world system, as the "Finalists" among the philosophers believe, nor is there the constant progress of which the "Moralists" speak, but there is an inexhaustible expression of life-energy which moves us and the world in a constant renewal of its elements. This renewal, this never ending creation is an end in itself. It expresses itself in us through the joy we experience during every moment in which we use our creative ability. Bergson arrives at a beautifully worded conclusion: "Celui qui est sûr, absolument sûr, d'avoir produit oeuvre viable et durable, celui-là n'a plus que faire de l'éloge, et se sent au-dessus de la gloire, parcequ'il est créateur, parcequ'il le sait, et parceque la joie qu'il en éprouve est une joie divine."[3]

Expressive in painting

If we now look at the most spiritual expressions of modern art, we shall find that the question of an end to the individual, the nation, the race or mankind is no longer a problem, because no final end is ever possible; instead, the theme is frequently the birth of life-giving forces, their transference to other parts of the cosmos, the constant change from one form into another, the connection between man and cosmos in the same rhythm, the creative energy, or the cause of this rhythm.

Let us take an example from modern poetry. It may be considered absurd to try to indicate the peculiar qualities of the spirit of our age by one illustration, but if the poet is a great one and if it would be impossible to imagine the subject he deals with at any other time than ours, we may be justified in considering it typical.

Robinson Jeffers places in the center of his narrative poem, "The Loving Shepherdess,"[4] a description of the happy life of the unborn child — the unborn as the speaker was in her mother's womb and the unborn in her own body:

> Have you never seen in your visions
> The golden country that our souls came from,
> Before we looked at the moon and stars and knew
> They are not perfect? We came from a purer peace

3. A short résumé of Bergson's philosophy is given in André Maurois's *Etudes littéraires, I;* 1941.
4. *Dear Judas and Other Poems,* 1929.

In a more perfect heaven; where there was nothing
But calm delight, no cold, no sickness, no sharp hail,
The haven of neither hunger nor sorrow,
But all-enfolding love and unchangeable joy
Near the heart of life . . .

The place was my mother's body before
I was born. You may remember it a little but I've
Remembered plainly: and the wailing pain of entering this air.
I've thought and thought and remembered. I found
A cave in a high cliff of white stone, when I was hiding from
people: It was there I had the first memory.
There I'd have stayed in the safe darkness forever; the sheep
were hungry and strayed out, so I couldn't stay . . .

When I was in my worst trouble
I knew that the child was feeding on peace and happiness. I had happiness
here in my body. It is not mine,
But I am its world and the sky around it, its loving God. It is having the prime
and perfect of life,
The nine months that are better than the ninety years . . .

And could the belief in constant change, in a sustaining creative energy,
instead of in death as the end, be better expressed than in the words of
the woman's counterpart in the same poem, the strange seer Vasquez?

Who was the spendthrift sowed them all over the sky, indistin-
guishable innumerable
Fish-scales of light? They drew together as they drifted away no path down the
wild darkness; he saw
The webs of their rays made them one tissue, their rays that were their very
substance and power filled wholly
The space they were in, so that each one touched all, there was no division
between them, no emptiness, and each
Changed substance with all the others and became the others. It was dreadful
to see
No space between them, no cave of peace nor no night of quietness, no blind
spot nor no deaf heart, but the tides
Of power and substance flood every cranny; no annihilation; no escape but
change; it must endure itself
Forever. It has the strength to endure itself. . . .

Next let us try to realize how the painters handle these themes. The
beginnings of life occupied Diego Rivera extensively in his Detroit mu-
rals, as far as was possible in frescoes devoted to the industrial development of a city. He depicts the changes in the cells of the human body
when they are affected by fertile or poisonous substances, the influence of

chemical products on the life of the child and the development of the embryo.

But of even more fundamental character is the representation of vital energies working towards the creation of life in abstract paintings by Klee, Kandinsky, Miro, Matta and others, or in the symbolic paintings of Tobey and Graves. The unfolding of energies in the growth of organic and inorganic life on earth and in the cosmos has been the subject of some of the most moving compositions of Klee. Mark Tobey shows the endless streams of energies flowing in different strengths and directions through the cosmos in his composition *World Egg* (Fig. 134), while Morris Graves is fond of showing the transformation from one substance to another in the life of birds and fish, of plants and minerals (Fig. 135). None of the best modern painters show death or decay except in connection with a new beginning of life or as a transitory stage to a more beautiful existence.

in sculpture Turning to sculpture, we have seen how much the sculptors of our time are interested in what was formerly called the lower forms of life, in animals like reptiles and fish which were among the first to inhabit the earth. Brancusi shows the beginning of organic life in his egg-shaped forms (Fig. 136). Flannagan has created more than once the moment when life penetrated the shell of the egg and produced an animal out of seemingly inorganic materials (Fig. 137). In his last, beautiful composition he shows the creation of human life: the birth of the child which rests peacefully between the legs of the mother (Fig. 138). In Henry Moore's art, the human beings are developing from the first unconscious state of mind into reality, their transformation from earth to life being hardly completed; while Lipchitz' bodies appear as if they had just been created out of earth by God's hands, carrying with them still all the qualities of earth in their heavy, massive shapes. The most characteristic expression of active life-energy penetrating into the body and pressing violently through its veins is seen in the art of Gaston Lachaise.

Creative energy is even more apparent in the content of abstract painting and sculpture. That abstract art is an essential part of the art expression of our time makes clear the importance we attach to the problems of the origin of life and of the belief that it can be found in the creative energies which initiate and sustain life. For the subject of abstract art is creative energy in its purest form. Like all art it is based upon observations made from nature. Abstract art follows the study of the creation of the cosmic world as we see it in the formation of new stars out of compact forms of nebulae, in the explosions of the sun or of meteors; or it results from the study of man-made machines, of motors creating energy, which

176

we have learned to admire in automobile plants, aeroplane factories and the engine rooms of ocean liners.

We do not need to understand these mechanisms in order to see the beauty of their continuous, forceful movements. Transferred into abstract art, the practical application of motor power is removed, and we see only the symbols of life-creating energies, the spirals and other elastic forms which convey the idea that everything, ourselves included, is a part of this life-creating rhythm. We find these life-enhancing qualities in the work of Moholy-Nagy, Archipenko, Gabo, Pevsner and other constructivists. As an example of the idea of growth expressed in abstract form, we reproduce one of Calder's mobiles, *Red Petals* (Fig. 139), in which we feel the leaves of flowers or trees shooting forward from a central source, filled to the brim in every line with life-energy.

How different are the expressions of the art of the Baroque age, for instance, from those of our time; we often find in Baroque sculpture representations of decayed bodies and skeletons, executed with morbid pleasure, or so-called "vanities," still lifes with skulls, which point to the terrible end of life. We cannot help but believe, after such a comparison, that a more exalted conception of life is dawning in the art of our own time.

According to this new concept God is no longer the God of revenge who rules the world of the Old Testament or primitive tribes; he is no longer the suffering God whose symbols belong to a past age, but is the creator and renovator of life, who has given us the gift of creating so that we may feel a connection with him. He is the God of work but also the God of love, because the aim of love is to create. The ultimate joy of woman is the creation of human beings; of man, creative spiritual work. Not all human beings are creative in the highest sense of the word, but every kind of labor, even the meanest, can be creative if conceived as such; it is all a necessary part of the constantly moving and changing world where even the greatest human creative energy is infinitely small. If we are conscious of the necessity to fulfill the work we are made for, in a world which lives because of energy, we shall be imbued with the vital impulse we need for the enjoyment of life. Happiness lies, not in the fulfillment of material wishes, or in a life of freedom and independence, but only in creative work.

Now that the best masters of our time have begun to show the way in their art, shall we not see the sculptors of the future erect monuments that will perfectly embody the new conception of an actual and spiritual reconstruction of life?

Acknowledgments are due, for advice and help in collecting material, to Walter C. Arensberg, Wayne Claxton, Ambrose Lansing, Karl Nierendorf, Walter Pach, Gisela M. Richter, Alden Smith, Curt Valentin; for correcting the manuscript, to Isabella Athey and Edith Ferry. I have learned a great deal from visiting studios of sculptors here and abroad; if only a few of these are mentioned by name in the text, it is because my intention has been, not to give a survey of modern sculptors, but to explain certain significant tendencies in contemporary sculpture.

Index of Artists

Other books and prints published by Wittenborn and Company.

Andre Masson: Mythology of Being. A poem, eight pen and ink drawings and a frontispiece. 200 numbered and signed copies. Large portfolio. 1942. Copies Nos. 1 to 30, with one additional original etching.

Georges Seurat by John Rewald. With 101 plates, 4 in color. Large 8vo. Rev. ed. 1946.

Georges Braque by A. E. Gallatin. With 12 plates and a color-facsimile frontispiece. 1943. 450 copies.

Georges Braque: Still Life, 1913. A color-facsimile reproduction in the original size, oval. 1943. 150 copies.

Ambroise Vollard: Editeur, 1867–1939. An appreciation and catalogue by *Una E. Johnson.* With 37 plates. 1944. 300 copies.

Line . . . Form . . . Color. Five woodblock color prints by *Louis Schanker.* Foreword by Carl Zigrosser. Large portfolio. 1944. 25 copies on Chinese rice paper.

Duchamp's Glass. An analytical reflection by *Katherine S. Dreier* and *Matta Echaurren.* With 5 plates. 8vo. 1944. 250 copies.

David Burliuk by Katherine S. Dreier. Foreword by Duncan Phillips. With 53 plates. 1944. Large 8vo.

Rainer Maria Rilke: The Sonnets to Orpheus. With nine engravings by *Kurt Roesch.* German-English text, M. D. Herter Norton translation. 35 numbered and signed copies on handmade paper from Arches, France. Folio. 1944.

Of Art . . . Plato to Picasso. Aphorisms and observations. Edited with contributions by *A. E. Gallatin.* 62 pp. 12 mo. 1944.

The Documents of Modern Art. Director: Robert Motherwell.

Guillaume Apollinaire: The Cubist Painters, aesthetic meditations, 1913. With 24 illustrations. Large 8vo. 1944.

Piet Mondrian: Plastic Art and Pure Plastic Art. With 24 illustrations, 2 color plates. Large 8vo. 1945.

L. Moholy-Nagy: The New Vision and *Abstract of an Artist.* With 73 illustrations. Large 8vo. 1946.

Problems of Contemporary Art.

No. 1: *Wolfgang Paalen: Form and Sense.* With 30 illustrations. Large 8vo. 1945.

W. R. Valentiner: Origins of Modern Sculpture. With 139 illustrations. Large 8vo. 1946.

Henry Moore: Shelter Sketch Book. With 80 illustrations. Large 8vo. 1945.

Paul Klee: A portfolio of ten color collotype plates of paintings. Introduction by Georg Schmidt. 1945.